I AM GODDESS

A Journey of Awakening

Rev. Natalie Haig

Copyright © 2017 by Rev. Natalie Haig

All rights reserved. No part of this book may be reproduced by any mechanical, photographic, or electronic process, or in the form of a phonographic recording; nor may it be stored in a retrieval system, transmitted, or otherwise be copied for public or private use – other than for "fair use" as brief quotations embodied in articles and reviews – without prior written permission of the author.

Published by: Sacred Breakthroughs. Distributed by Amazon.com

LIBRARY AND ARCHIVES CANADA CATALOGUING IN PUBLICATION
ISBN-13: 978-1976365706, E-book ISBN-10: 1976365708
Cover design: Jade & Opal Consulting Agency, Toronto, Ontario

Rev. Natalie Haig is the founder of Sacred Breakthroughs. She does not dispense medical advice or prescribe the use of any technique as a form of treatment for physical, emotional, spiritual or medical problems without the advice of a physician. This book is for informational purposes only. In the event you use any of the information in this book for yourself, which is your constitutional right, the author and the publisher assume no responsibility for your actions. For more information concerning this book, please visit: www.sacredbreakthroughs.com.

"A woman in harmony with her spirit is like a river flowing. She goes where she will without pretense and arrives at her destination prepared to be herself, and only herself."

- Maya Angelou

Contents

THE BEGINNING   i

SPECIAL THANKS   iii

PART I: **G**REATNESS   1

PART II: **O**VERCOMING   24

PART III: **D**ESERVING   51

PART IV: **D**IVINE   70

PART V: **E**MBRACING   99

PART VI: **S**TRENGTH   131

PART VII: **S**ENSUALITY   146

THE BEGINNING

"To have a breakthrough, you must consciously connect with the invisible forces that are everywhere around you, urging you to go beyond your old conditioning."   - Deepak Chopra

I believe we each have a Goddess within, and that this Goddess is a natural part of us, just as the sun is a part of the sky. She warms our hearts, feeds our souls, and awakens us to the Divine Feminine. She is the unconditional love we are each a part of.

We are each on different journeys, and it is important to remember that. We cannot compare ourselves to others, but instead, must embrace where we are on our paths. Some of us have already awakened to our Inner Goddess, and some of us are just stepping into our power. While others are unfolding, slowly but surely, in the direction of awakening the Goddess within, some may not yet be ready to, and it is all perfect. It is not a race. It is a beautiful unfoldment.

To me, it's a sacred journey that unfolds in its own perfect timing. We are each living our own story in this beautiful life. We are each learning, growing, and unfolding into the Divine Love Light within us, much like the Lotus Flower.

The Lotus is a beautiful flower, and it grows where people least expect it. It grows in mud, in darkness, in the shadows of the waters. What a blessing to see something so beautiful and sacred growing out of something dark and unpleasant! The Lotus teaches that we sometimes need to have some mud, pain, sadness, or difficulties in our lives in order to develop and express our strength and beauty.

This book tells of my journey – how I awakened to my Inner Goddess. It tells of my continuing journey — unfolding and blooming like the Lotus flower.

I wrote this book in my mind for years. I wanted to share my wisdom, but I wasn't ready to share my experiences. I was concerned about what others might think of me. I struggled with how to best say what I wanted to say. When I sat down to write it did not seem to flow. I set the book aside for a while and continued living my life.

Today, I am courageous, I am authentic, I do not take things personally and I am open to share from my heart. I believe everything always unfolds in its perfect time. I am now ready to share my Divine Journey. I hope that my story inspires, motivates, and awakens the part of you that is ready for a beautiful and powerful change.

SPECIAL THANKS

First of all, I would like to thank the Higher Power, which can be called many things: God, Source, The Universe, Creator, Divine Guidance and so on. I am a non-denominational minister who believes in a Higher Power. What each of us chose to call our Higher Power is perfect for us. We each experience our own realities and there is no wrong way. There is only your way for you, and my way for me. In these pages, I feel comfortable using the word God or Source interchangeably. When you see the word God in these pages, I am not referring to an old man sitting on a cloud. I am referring to the Divine Light, the Source of all, the Higher Power that guides us and surrounds us with love, no matter what.

I thank God, for giving me the desire and courage to tell my story. Thank you for all of the divine interventions that I see on a daily basis and for the unconditional love that I feel from you. I have always felt your presence in my heart and have received exactly what I've needed with every step of my journey.

A special thanks to my children for inspiring me to be more childlike and playful. They are full of joy, love, and silliness, which remind me not to take life too seriously. They teach me how to connect to my passion with patience, trust, and love. They teach me what unconditional love is really all about.

They each have their unique gifts and energies and model for me to be true to myself, no matter what. I thank my husband who believes in me and encourages me to be the best version of myself. He was the first person who fully understood me and my potential, even before I recognized it myself.

To all of my friends who believed in me, thank you. You know who you are. Our hearts and souls are connected in oneness, and I am truly grateful for your presence in my life. A BIG thanks to Rev. Julia Norris who has been there since the beginning. She is the expert who took my book under her wings and sprinkled some fairy dust on it, making it flow better by editing the book from her heart. I am so blessed to have her in my life. She showered me with kindness, grace, and support along the birthing of this book.

Last, but not the least, to my mother who taught me to be a leader and encourages me to follow my heart. Thank you Mom, for doing your best. I appreciate and love you more than I can express in words.

PART I

GREATNESS

"As human beings, our greatness lies not so much in being able to remake the world - that is the myth of the atomic age - as in being able to remake ourselves." — *Mahatma Gandi*

There are many things in life that can be labeled as "great" or "having greatness." However, the Greatness I am referring to is not found on the outside, such as money, big houses, or other material goods. The Greatness I am referring to can't be bought. It has no physical form. We can only find it inside ourselves. It is found within our hearts, in our souls, and in our connection to our Source. It is in the Higher Power that created us all. We connect to our Greatness through the awareness that there is more to life than meets the eye and feeling a strong desire to live your life to the fullest. This divine Greatness is the real YOU.

Source

Yes, I believe in God, The Universe - our Source. I am not preaching religion, as I believe we each have our own sacred way of connecting with Source. The name we choose to call that Higher Power does not matter. It is the Greatness all around us that blankets us with divine love and light and embraces us with miracles and blessings.

I was drawn to study metaphysical science in my mid-twenties and to learn about the Oneness of Presence. To me, "Oneness of Presence" means the connections we have with ourselves, with our awareness of life, and with our Source.

Staying connected to your heart is the best way to fully embrace this Oneness. We must listen to our truth and our own passion, for each of us has greatness to share with others. Some people call this Greatness a "purpose," "an inner calling," "a blueprint," or "a personal legend." Most of us strive to follow our Greatness. We may find ourselves asking questions such as, "Who am I?" "Why am I here?" "What is my purpose in life?" and "Who or what is God?"

After years of exploring different religions, I discovered that the core of each is the same: Connecting to the Higher Power through love. Ultimately, we all want to be happy, feel loved, and find peace. When we let go of labels and masks and remember that we are all the same, we experience an awareness that words cannot describe. We are all connected, even though it seems that we are separate and living in our own realities!

One of the Greatnesses in life is that we are all One. As Dr. Wayne Dyer often reminded us, "We are all spiritual beings having a human experience." Once we can embrace this truth, we will find ourselves accepting our circumstances more easily, we will love more easily, and we will be more easily loved.

When we become aware, we will feel that God is in our hearts, and we are never truly alone. Since God is our Creator, we are a part of God, just as we created our children, and they are a part of us. We are all connected, because we came from the same Oneness, the same Source.

With a connection to God in your heart, anything is possible. I talk to God on a daily basis. Not just once a day, such as at the end of the day. I talk to God, the angels, and my guides as if they are right beside me, because I feel they are. When I am showering, when I am driving the kids to school, when I am on my way to work, when I am in nature, while I cook, and even sometimes while making love. ("Thank you God for this amazing man!") I believe the more we connect to the Divine Power, to our Source, the more we begin to see the magic, miracles, divine interventions, and blessings in our lives.

Greatness can be found everywhere we look. We can connect to Greatness in nature, through other people, and even through animals. I know you may be thinking that you've heard all of this before, and you probably have. Many teachers are giving the same messages about one love, manifesting our realities, following our hearts, and being happy. We each offer our own insights, our own energy, and our unique experiences that will resonate with whoever needs the information at this time.

For example, there are many places where you can eat ice cream. In my neighborhood, I can choose either Baskin Robbins or Dairy Queen, and sometimes I feel like having one over the other. Or I may choose frozen yogurt, instead, which is worth the 20 minutes drive. The ice cream vendor or frozen treat I choose is decided by what I feel drawn to in that moment. So, it really doesn't matter how many places sell the same product or how many books talk about God or positive energy. In the end, the flavor, or the unique energy that each book radiates, will draw you to it.

We all want to be surrounded with love and happiness. I have many clients who come to me from all walks of life, both men and women, and say things like, "I forgot how it feels to be happy," "All I want is to be happy," and "I need to stop taking things seriously and start feeling happy."

Being optimistic, grateful, happy, and joyous, is an art. It is part of our journey to learn this art; to learn to embrace the Greatness that life offers us.

Good Company

One of the Greatnesses in life is that we all have the power to change the energy that surrounds us. Have you ever been in the company of someone who is very positive? Or the opposite, someone who is always negative? Have you noticed how you feel in their company? Long ago, Mark Twain advised that we "Keep away from people who try to belittle your ambitions. Small people always do that, but the really great make you feel that you, too, can become great."

A hot cup of tea or an ice-cold glass of water will either change or stay the same, based on its surrounding. Its temperature will rise or fall to match the temperature around it. It is the same with our personal energy. Our personal energy can be influenced by the energy around us. Being around negative people can affect our energy and leave us feeling drained, while positive people can increase our positive energy and leave us feeling energized and joyful. Which person would you prefer to spend more time with? I prefer the positive, upbeat person who encourages me and affirms that I can be, do, or have anything I desire.

I do my best to surround myself with good, positive company. This includes attending classes, workshops, seminars and other gatherings of people with similar views about life, dreams, and ideals. I enjoy attending such events, because they nourish my soul, my core. These events inspire me to continue pursing my dream of being on a large venue stage one day — shining and sharing my positive energy with others.

We become like that which we surround ourselves with. When we surround ourselves with love and light, we become that love and light. What we focus on expands. When we focus on love and positive thoughts and fill our lives with what makes us feel happy, we increase our energy and ultimately vibrate at a higher frequency where we can find our truth. Your truth is your passion and the core of who you are. My passion is sharing unconditional love and light with others by inspiring, encouraging, and being of service to others.

Everything Is Energy

Science tells us that everything is energy. Everything that exists is made up of energy as its most basic level. The earth, our food, our water, even our music. Everything we know and interact with has its own energy frequency, or vibration. Every person you meet also has his or her own energy frequency, or vibration. The universe all around us is energy.

This is how I explain the energy of crystals in my holistic classes: Look around you. Do you believe that the earth is alive? Food and water keep us alive. That means the source of our food and water – Mother Earth, is alive, too. The earth, and everything in the earth, has its own specific frequency of energy. We can use this energy to heal ourselves. The energy of crystals can be used to help balance out our own energy.

If you ever feel flustered, anxious, overwhelmed, or any unwanted emotion, just step outside for a few minutes, and stand barefoot on the earth. Closing your eyes, take three to ten deep breaths and FEEL your feet against the earth. Feel the warmth or coolness. Feel the texture of the surface under your feet. As you focus your attention on your feet connecting to the earth, you will begin to connect to the energy frequency of the earth. The earth's energy frequency will begin to positively affect your energy frequency and bring your energy back to its normal vibration.

If you like, you can take it even further. As you stand still and quiet, imagine that you are a tree with roots growing out of the soles of your feet. These roots will help you feel more grounded in your own power, rather than at the mercy of your unwanted emotions. Next, imagine your roots extending down through the layers of the earth, branching out in all directions, going deeper and deeper. See a root reaching out and wrapping around a big, brilliant pink stone – a rose quartz crystal. Rose quartz has a calming energy and is known as the stone of peace and unconditional love.

As the root wraps around the Rose Quartz, see the energy of peace and unconditional love pulsing in the stone. Watch the Rose Quartz share its peaceful, loving energy, as you see a pink pulsating light travel from the stone, into the root. Watch the pink pulsating energy travel up the roots, all the way back up through the layers of the earth, and into the soles of your feet. Feel the peaceful, unconditional love flowing into your body as it enters the soles of your feet. Watch as your body slowly fills to the top of your head with this peaceful, loving energy. Know that every cell and molecule is filling with this peace and unconditional love.

As we take a few moments to consciously connect with Mother Earth and feel our feet on the grass, we change our energy fields. This simple activity helps us ground and center, regain our emotional footing, and return us to our true selves. It helps us let go of the unwanted feelings and fills our bodies with LOVE. We are so blessed. We can connect like a plug into the Earth's energy and immediately feel better anytime we like.

Sharing Love

When we connect with love to others, we are recognizing the Greatness within them. We often hear people say "Namaste," which means, "The Divine in me recognizes the Divine in you." What if, instead of just saying "Namaste," we lived "Namaste?" Taking the time to truly connect with others, to recognize the Divine in others, is very important for both parties.

In a world where technology is number one, we connect via Facebook, Twitter, and e-mails, and start to lose our personal connection. The most important connections we can have with one another is heart to heart connections, through our physical form by love, hugs, and truly listening to others. With all of the technology and other distractions around us, sometimes we don't really listen. Instead, we may be thinking about how we are going to respond when it's our turn to talk, what we are doing later that evening, or we may be trying to discretely check our texts.

To truly listen to others – to still our minds and listen to their words, their body language, and to feel their presence – is a pure expression of love. Providing the space of being truly heard gives the other person space to blossom. It builds trust, strengthens relationships, and is a powerful tool for healing.

When we express our love to others, the expression of love will also cycle back to us. What goes around comes around. Saying "I love you" will inspire others to say, "I love you" in return.

My husband and I say "I love you" every morning, throughout the day via text messaging, as part of our greeting when he gets home from work, and then again before we go to sleep. We make a point to not take each other for granted and consciously express our love for and appreciation of each other.

Another way to share love is by noticing others and offering compliments about what you appreciate about them. As we go through our day, it costs us nothing, not even time, to say a kind word to someone, but each kind word is priceless. Who knows? Maybe that one compliment is exactly what the person needs to hear at this time.

One day, when I was picking up my son from pre-school, I happened across his teacher. I told her she was awesome for taking the time to teach the children and to help them make crafts for Mother's Day. I said, "You are amazing! Look at everything you do for them! He loves coming here! What an awesome job you are doing!"

With tears in her eyes she said, "I needed to hear that. Thank you. Sometimes it's hard to do it all – the crafts, play, the cleaning up. Excuse the mess."

"I don't mind the mess," I told her. That's how we know the children are having fun! It's supposed to be messy!" The teacher confided in me that this day she had been feeling overwhelmed, and she thanked me for making her day. Just a simple acknowledgment had totally changed her state of mind and relieved the day's worth of stress she had been feeling. What a gift!

On an episode of "The View," the panel was talking about President Obama's family life. They were telling about the family's dinnertime tradition called "Roses and Thorns." Each shares one good thing that happened or one thing that made them feel grateful; this was the "rose." Each also shared one thing that made them upset, sad or unhappy, which was the "thorn." A practice such as this can foster communication, as well as teach children to focus on the positive, even in the middle of unhappy situations.

Loving the idea, I incorporated it into our family's dinnertime, as well. Doing this every evening provides everyone an opportunity to share his or her feelings and thoughts, and allows everyone to celebrate the "roses" and express compassion for the "thorns."

Letting Go of Your Stones

Harboring negative thoughts is like carrying a backpack full of stones. Individually, each stone seems insignificant in size and weight. However, as they accumulate in the backpack, they become heavy. Wearing the heavy backpack, hour after hour, day after day, becomes exhausting.

Negative thoughts affect us the same way. Negative thoughts have a lower vibration, which affects our personal vibration. The energetic affect makes us feel drained and weighed down. It dulls our thoughts and creates imbalance. When we constantly entertain negative thoughts, we are constantly adding more "stones" to our "backpacks." Over time, the collection of negative thoughts we hold onto will cause us to create a life full of heaviness, sorrow, pity, negativity, and disease.

We have all "worn a backpack of stones," because society trained us to do so. Fortunately, we do not have to. We have other options. We have the power to carry anything we want on our journey. We have the power to choose our thoughts. We can empty that backpack. We can dump those heavy stones in a garden and fill the backpack with "flowers" of positive thoughts.

Positive thoughts have a higher vibration that complements our natural vibration. They enhance joy, peace, and love in our lives. Even just imagining positive thoughts as vibrant, light, and colorful flowers can positively affect our vibration. The weight of a backpack filled with flowers would be hardly noticeable.

The next time a negative thought shows up, we can say to ourselves: "I choose to carry flowers instead of stones. I choose to let this go." Establishing a habit of doing this will allow us to feel more positive each day and live a happier life.

Thoughts Become Things

Everything we see started as a thought before it showed up in physical form. Thoughts are energy, and the more energy we put into a thought by thinking it, the closer we get to having the essence of that thought show up in our physical reality. When we focus on a thought and take inspired action, we create our own realities.

Think of a computer, for example. Someone thought about creating a computer. They thought about it, imagined it, and then took action by building components, testing equipment, putting electrical circuits together, and so on. All of these actions created the base for the computers that many of us own today. This person didn't stop at the thought, "I should make a computer." He was inspired to take action.

We are all powerful creators. We all have the ability to manifest our dreams by living from our Greatness, our extraordinary energy in life. Because our thoughts have the potential of manifesting into our physical realities, being mindful of our thoughts is very important to living a balanced life. Negative thoughts have the same potential as positive thoughts, so it is wise to be conscious of our thoughts and spend time thinking the positive ones instead of the negative ones.

When we are in sync with Source, we become open to receive all of the magic and blessings we desire. Taking the time to be in alignment with Source is positive action that will move us toward achieving our goals. I often have experiences thinking something and having it happen, sometimes as soon as on the same day. Here is an example:

One morning, I was driving with my kids, on the way back from a visit with my mother, listening to the radio. The radio host said, "Congratulations, you are caller number 30! You have won two tickets to see Bruno Mars in concert this Saturday!" The caller was very excited.

I thought, "That would be great if I could go to see Bruno Mars. I am free this Saturday." It was a fleeting thought. I didn't dwell on any negative aspects— I didn't have a ticket, and I likely wouldn't be listening to the radio the next time the station invited callers to try to win tickets. I didn't think anymore about it. I let it go. Later that evening, my sister-in-law called me. "Are you free this Saturday?" she asked. "I have an extra Bruno Mars ticket. I was planning to go with Mom, but I don't want to go anymore. You can go with her if you want." I was excited and my voice was full of joy. I said, "I was just thinking about that today! Yes, I am free! Thank you so much! I can't wait! What a nice surprise!"

My kids think I have magical powers because these things happen so often for me. I keep telling them that what you focus on expands, and when you focus on good feelings and thoughts, you get more things in your life that make you feel good. The same is true for the opposite: when you focus on the negative, you will get more things in your life that make you feel negative. My kids understand and are doing their best to consciously create their own realities.

To become a conscious creator of your reality, start by paying attention to your thoughts. Awareness is the key. Start keeping a journal. Write down your thoughts each night and reflect upon them. Are your thoughts mostly optimistic or pessimistic? Are you thinking more about what you want or what you don't want? With awareness you can begin to create a change. As you become aware of your thoughts, you can make a conscious choice to change your thoughts in the middle of the thought. Eventually, you may notice that negative, unwanted thoughts rarely enter your mind at all. Changing habits of thinking is possible, though it will take time. There is no quick and easy fix, so be gentle and patient with yourself.

Perception Controls Reality

"If you change the way you look at things, the things you look at change."
— Dr. Wayne Dyer

It's easy to get caught up in a negative point of view, especially when things aren't going the way we wish in our lives. We are quick to judge things as "good" and "bad," "wanted" and "unwanted." However, if we look back at our lives, we frequently discover that those "hard" times were the catalysts we needed for growth. If we had been able to avoid the difficulties, we would not be as wise as we are today. Everything comes to us for a reason— for our good—and when we judge something as "bad," we slow down the "good" that it showed up to deliver. In the middle of a challenge, if we can ask, "What if this is showing up to help me?" that question can be exactly what we need to be able to release our resistance. It can also open our eyes to see the good that is hidden in the trial.

When we look at things with positive thoughts and an attitude of gratitude, we can see the magic and beauty that fills our lives. Even in the middle of difficulties, there is always a way to change how we are looking at things. Allowing ourselves to see beyond the struggles and see what is going right can change our perspective when we face the struggles again.

When we walk with a divine awareness of love, things seem so much brighter and lighter. Every day is an opportunity to do something that makes us feel good. Every day, do your best to smile more, laugh more, and consciously feel joy and positive energy surrounding you.

Gratitude

"If the only prayer you said in your whole life was 'thank you,' that would suffice."   *- Meister Eckhart*

Another important gift we can give ourselves is having an attitude of gratitude. Appreciating everything that we have in life is important for our well-being. Appreciation is a high-frequency energy that affects not just the one appreciating, but everyone and everything around us. It has a ripple effect. When we are grateful, we radiate love, positive energy, and abundance. Through our gratitude, we send positive energy into the Universe.

Gratitude also keeps us open to receiving more blessings into our lives. When we appreciate, we are inviting Source to grace us with more to appreciate. Expressing gratitude, whether verbally or silently, tells the Universe that we are open to receive more blessings, more love, and more positive energy into our lives. The energy of gratitude acts like a magnet and attracts more good things to us. We need to always show our appreciation for everything and everyone we have in our lives.

Imagine opening a gift and just shrugging it off with a neutral look on your face, not showing any enthusiasm or appreciation for the gift. What do you think might happen? The person who gave you the gift will see that you are not grateful and will probably not want to give you a gift again. In the opposite scenario, if you expressed gratitude, with a smile or some enthusiasm, and said "thank you," the giver would be more likely to give you another gift in the future. Your gratitude infuses both of you with positive energy, and the ripple effect will leave both of you feeling good.

Each morning I tell Source "thank you" for all of my blessings — my children, my home, my ability to see all of the beauty life offers me, my mental and physical health, waking up to enjoy the fresh air every morning, and the unconditional love that I feel on a daily basis. Saying "thank you" is very powerful. Practice saying "thank you" every day to Source, to family, to friends, and even to strangers.

Giving

We have all heard the expression, "It is more blessed to give than to receive." However, there are two sides to that coin. For there to be a giver, there must also be a receiver. Both positions are equally important and necessary. Without one, the other cannot exist. I do not believe that one is better than the other, for they each hold their own blessing.

When we give to others from a place of love, we receive more love. When we open our hearts to send love, we heal ourselves and each other. However, if we give something out of a sense of obligation, or with any other negativity, such as pity or guilt, the result is more negativity. The energy behind the giving is what really matters.

When we give from the high-frequency of love, we are of service to others. Not just through our gift, whether it is a thing or our time, but also through the positive energy we radiate. It is important that we always feel good in our hearts when we give to someone else. If it does not feel good to give, then giving is not the right choice in that moment.

We are often encouraged to give from a place of feeling sorry for another person or situation. When we give from a place of pity, we empower and validate that low-frequency energy. Doing this negatively affects both the giver and the receiver, as we energetically agree with the "helpless victim" state. By agreeing in this way, the other person stays stuck in the low- frequency energy, and we invite low-frequency situations into our lives. I am not saying not to give to those in need, I am saying, check your intention and only give from a place of love. If you feel called to help someone in need, then help, but do so out of love, not out of pity.

Giving from obligation is another pitfall we often fall into. This is one of the main reasons for holiday stress—buying gifts for people because we feel we must. Aunt Susie sent a Christmas card, so I must send one to her. The neighbor gave us a loaf of homemade banana bread, so now she is on my shopping list. On and on it goes. Obligation giving isn't limited to holidays. The offering plate is passed at the church. The homeless person on the corner has no food. Giving from a sense of obligation has low-frequency energy. There is no joy in this kind of giving. Giving from obligation shifts our energy into a more "victim" state, as we are feeling a sense of "no choice" in our sense of obligation. We can feel the difference between this kind of giving and giving with compassion.

We must pay attention to how it feels when we give. If it feels good, give. If it does not, then do not give. The way we feel is how we know if giving in this situation is going to be the best action for all. Giving from our hearts, from a place of love, allows that love to spread to others, and that's the only time that it is good to give.

Touchstones of Gratitude

"Gratitude is the most important emotion for humans to experience. It changes your body, emotions, and your mind. When you are grateful, stress disappears. When you are grateful, fear disappears. When you are grateful, you feel rich inside."   - *Tony Robbins*

Keeping a Gratitude Journal is helpful for staying in alignment with our Greatness. Writing down the feelings, blessings, and miracles that we have experienced helps us focus our attention on our abundance and attract even greater abundance into our lives. Having a tangible reminder that we can refer back to helps keep us in sync with our Greatness.

I started keeping a journal in my late teens. I recorded in my journal all the great things that happened to me each day – Spirit encounters, predictions, manifestations, miracles, and divine interventions. While writing, I was able to relive the events and recreate the emotional feelings that happened as the events occurred. By noticing the events, remembering them, writing them down, and then later reading about them again, I maintained a high level of positive energy. By feeling good and appreciating all that had happened, I attracted more events into my life that created the same kinds of feelings. It was a perpetual cycle of good feelings and good feeling events!

A similar activity is keeping a gratitude jar. Each day, make a note of something that makes you feel grateful, and place it in the jar. Periodically, open the jar and read all of the notes. This is a nice activity that the whole family can become involved in. My children and I do this, and they love it!

Taking it a step further, you could start a gratitude club where you and your friends make a list, one item per day; of things you are grateful for, then meet once a month and share your list.

My friends and I did a similar activity during the Christmas season one year. Each of us had a small box. We each wrote down a positive message or something we appreciated about the others in the group—one note for each member. We then put our "love note" into the appropriate box. Afterward, we read and shared our messages with each other. It felt so nice to hear all the positive reinforcement from each other. Now, if ever one of us is feeling down, we can just open our little box and read the messages to ourselves. We will instantly feel better, because the love in the notes is like medicine that soothes. The high frequency of love that these notes carry will help balance our energy.

Every night I make a mental list of things that makes me feel grateful. I acknowledge my blessings, because the more I recognize that my life is an abundance of blessings, the more energy I return to Source. Source will continue to give me more things that will make me feel grateful. It's a continuous cycle of love!

The Effect of Thoughts

Dr. Masaru Emoto studied the effect of words on water. He devised experiments in which bottles of water were exposed to specific words or phrases, such as "love," "thank you," "you are beautiful," "hate," "you fool," "I will kill you," and more. Other bottles of water were exposed to different types of music or to prayers. The water was then frozen and viewed under a high-power microscope. Under a microscope, the water, though taken from the same source, formed crystals that varied in aesthetics. Water exposed to kind words, prayers, or gentle, positive music formed breathtakingly beautiful crystals. The water exposed to unkind words and harsh music formed crystals that appeared distorted, and some formed no crystals at all. These experiments suggest that our thoughts, intentions, and words have a powerful effect on water's crystalline structure. What a profound idea to contemplate, considering the human body is made of approximately 70% water.

These experiments show us that our thoughts truly do affect our bodies. If we stayed in a state of gratitude on a daily basis, imagine how amazing our bodies would feel! We would feel vibrant, happy, and full of positivity. If we tell ourselves things like, "'I am enough!" "I am beautiful!" "I love myself!"

"My body is healthy and strong!" and "I can achieve anything!" Then we will be helping our bodies to be healthier, and the water molecules in our bodies will be infused with love – crystal clear love! This is yet another reason that having an attitude of gratitude is important.

The Power of Words

We want our lives to be filled with blessings and positive energy. One way to attract blessings and positive energy is by paying attention to what we think and say. Our words are very powerful. We must remember to choose our words wisely.

Words are like seeds of magic. With our words, we can make someone feel better, build up their self-esteem, or comfort them, all the while, making them feel loved. At the same time, with our words, we can tear someone down, destroy them, and dim their light. We have so much power with our words alone, whether spoken or thought. We can use our words to nurture others to become strong, loving beings, or we can poison them with negative, false truths.

PART II

OVERCOMING

"You may encounter many defeats, but you must not be defeated. Please remember that your difficulties do not define you. They simply strengthen your ability to overcome."   *- Maya Angelou*

Life is like a school: full of lessons, tests, and time on the playground. Each hardship that comes our way is an opportunity for us to learn and grow. Though we may be afraid or angry during difficult times, we can usually see the value in the struggle once we make it through the darkness and look for the hidden gift the struggle held. I am grateful to have experienced all of my struggles, because they have molded me into the strong Goddess that I am today.

Pruning a rose bush by cutting off some of the branches allows the bush to redirect its life force and grow healthier and stronger and produce more blossoms. Similarly, sometimes we need pruning. Sometimes we need possessions, situations, or people to be removed from our lives in order for us to become the fullest, truest version of ourselves we were intended to be.

We often resist these growing pains and try to cling to "what was," because we cannot see the beauty of who we are becoming that lies around the bend, just out of sight.

Because it is easy to get lost in the struggle and challenges and lose focus, I want to encourage you in your struggles by sharing mine with you. The struggles, the growth, and the diamond I become as I make it through to the other side. What I am about to share with you, even some members of my family do not know. I have kept it private until now. It's very personal, yet I feel it is important to share.

I want you to know that no matter your background, no matter what you have gone through, and no matter what others may say about you, you can overcome every barrier that is hindering you. You are not what has happened to you, and you do not have to define yourself by your experiences. Your future is not determined by your past. No matter what has happened, you can create the life you desire. I know you can, because I did.

I believe that everything I have experienced has happened to support me and make me who I am today. I am grateful to have the chance to share with you the treasures that came from the darkest times of my life. Here is the story of my journey:

Being Bullied and Abused

From grade two to grade seven, I was bullied by my classmates on a regular basis. My classmates would form a circle around me and chant, "Oh, look! Natalie is going to cry! Watch! She is going to cry! Cry, Natalie! Cry!"

With big smiles on their faces, they laughed and chanted, and of course, I would cry. I was ashamed that they could make me cry, but I could not stop myself. It was as if someone had turned on a water tap. I could not make them stop taunting me, and the teachers were oblivious. I became the entertainment for my classmates. They would surround me and tell me to cry, and I would. I felt weak and afraid and humiliated. I dreaded going outside for recess. I frequently hid in a bathroom stall; my feet curled up under me, as I perched on the toilet, hoping no one would find me.

I especially hated reading in front of the class. My classmates watching me made me feel that I was, once again, at their mercy. I became anxious and felt like crying. They had conditioned me to cry simply from their collective gaze. Young, shy, and powerless, I let them walk all over me. I allowed them to strip me of my personal power. Because of their constant treatment, I became shy, insecure, and depressed.

At home, it wasn't any better. My stepfather was an alcoholic and was very abusive. He was short-tempered and routinely gave my mother black eyes. When I did anything wrong, or if he even thought I had done something wrong, it became an excuse to hit me. It was an extremely dysfunctional household. Each day was like walking on eggshells. One minute everyone was happy, because the adults each had a joint in their hands. The next minute, my stepfather would be yelling, and my mother would be screaming for her life. I was terrified in my own home. Sometimes, I imagined that I had another family. I daydreamed that if I could have been switched at birth, I would be living with a different and happy family. I loved my mother and my siblings, but I didn't feel loved in my household.

I was always afraid and felt like I didn't belong anywhere. Neither school nor home was a good place for me to be. I didn't feel safe anywhere. I didn't want to live like this anymore, but I had no choice. I was trapped. I became withdrawn and extremely quiet, pouring myself into books, praying for a way out of this nightmare.

One day, I was upstairs in my bedroom and heard my mother screaming, "You are killing me!" she cried. I flew down the staircase like Wonder Woman, passing over all the steps in two huge leaps. I ran into the kitchen and saw my stepfather beating my mother with a large, heavy wooden chair. She was as helpless as a drowning infant as he beat her over the head and back with the chair. All she could do was cover her face with her arms and wait for him to stop.

Suddenly, from out of nowhere, a powerful, booming voice yelled, "Stop it! You're killing her! I'm calling the police!"

The voice sounded familiar. I realized: that was ME! That was MY powerful, booming voice! I had no idea I had that kind of strength inside me. I was surprised at myself for harnessing my anger and taking such powerful action. I then ran to the phone, called 9-1-1, and told them what was happening. This was the first time I had touched my inner Goddess as a teenager.

We lived in the projects, in low-income townhouses. At the sound of sirens pulling into our complex, the neighbors and their kids poured out of their homes to watch the show they knew would follow. A group of about thirty people gathered around the scene, gawking at the wild man yelling and swearing as the police wrestled him to the ground to handcuff him.

Belly down, my stepfather repeatedly smashed his face into the cement sidewalk next to the parking area, bloodying his face with each hit, yelling at the police to stop beating him. To protect him from further injuring himself, the police had to pin him down, pressing his face hard against the pavement. After handcuffing him, the police picked him up, put him in the squad car, and drove away.

I looked at my mother. She looked terrible, but I was just happy she was alive. She had huge bruises on her neck and back, and her body was swollen like a party balloon from the beating. She was barely able to walk; yet she refused to go to the hospital. Her ability to endure such pain was also her downfall, because it prevented her from asking for help.

The beatings from my stepfather were regular events. The neighbors knew what was happening in my house, but no one ever did anything. No one talked about it to me or asked if we were okay. Maybe they didn't care. Maybe they were scared to get involved. Who knows why? I never spoke to anyone about it, because I was scared, myself. It was as if there was a silent agreement among the neighborhood to protect our secret. I was living a nightmare. Everyone knew it, but no one helped. I felt alone in the middle of the small community that heard every crash and bang.

That day, something in me changed. I saw how pathetic a man could be. I saw how I could stand in my power and make a difference. I knew that I was the reason my mother was still alive; I had saved her life.

I thought for sure that my mother would file for a divorce from that monster after this. But she didn't. She was caught in a cycle that is typical of abusive relationships. He once again told her, "I'm sorry. I promise I will never do this again." She once again forgave him, and let him back into our home for the same scene to be repeated the following month.

I couldn't take it anymore. I knew I couldn't keep our secret any longer, and I knew my heart couldn't bear to watch my mother be beaten any more. I didn't know what else to do, so I opened up to my guidance counselors at school. The counselors told me that since I was only fifteen years old, they had to call Family and Children Services. I was scared. I loved my mother and didn't want us to be taken away from her; I just wanted us all to be safe from my stepfather.

Family and Children Services came to our house. My mother lied to the social worker, saying she had broken up with my stepfather. The social worker believed her and left. I was relieved when I learned that the case had been closed and that my siblings and I were able to stay with my mother.

My mother was angry with me for years, because I shared our secret with my counselors. She called me a big mouth, and scolded and belittled me for speaking up. I felt all alone and ashamed, like I did something wrong.

I then retreated inward. I prayed every chance I had. I just couldn't understand why I was with this family. I felt like I didn't belong anywhere. I created a fantasy life in my head. I imagined flying on a Pegasus into a fairytale land. I had magical powers that could teleport me into a new, far away heaven. In order to survive the ongoing abuse I lived in, I spent a lot of time in my far away heaven.

Eventually, my mother did get a divorce. Not because of the abuse, but because she learned my stepfather was cheating on her. Ten years of abuse had finally ended for me!

I didn't want to end up with a life like my mother had, so I promised myself I would do my best everyday to improve myself. I promised myself that I would choose a different path and a different kind of relationship.

Seeking Truth and Fighting Fear

Once my mother left my stepfather, I was happy to finally have some peace in my home. The chaos and turmoil had ended, but I knew there was something that was still not right. It seemed there was something missing in my life. It was then that I started seeking my truth. Who am I? Why had all of this happened to me? What is my purpose in life? I needed to know.

I began looking for answers. Because I was being bullied at my Catholic school, I did not want to find my answers in the Catholic religion. I thought, "If the Catholic children are mean and bulling me, then I do not want to be Catholic." Instead, I looked elsewhere. I attended Christian Bible studies. It made me feel good learning that Jesus and God really loved me. I liked feeling loved. It was a comforting, yet foreign, concept to consider after the years of abuse I had endured. However, I also learned that I needed to be afraid. I learned I needed to fear the unseen. I learned that evil spirits were "out there" and were trying to "get me." I began to fear that a monster was going to come or something bad was going to happen to me in the dark.

I didn't understand the fear. I had seen spirits before, when I was younger. They felt comforting, not frightening. They hadn't seemed evil. I also remembered that when I was around sixteen years old, I had told my doctor about the spirits that I had seen. The doctor told me they weren't real and that I needed to start thinking with the logical part of my mind. He wanted to prescribe medication, but I refused. Confused, I shared my experience with the Bible studies teacher. She told me it was the devil playing tricks on me.

  Once again, I felt scared, lost, and confused. I would pray every night for an answer. I was even confused about prayer, now. I would say, "In the name of the Father, the Son, and the Holy Spirit. If I said this wrong, please, God forgive me. I am confused. I'm not sure which religion is right. I'm not sure about anything anymore. I'm not sure how to pray. Please stop letting me see these spirits. I am scared. I do not like feeling scared. Please show me my way. Who am I? Why am I here? I do not want to live with fear anymore. Please take my pain away. I need help!"

  I developed a phobia of the dark, because whenever it was dark, I would still see spirits. They never did anything except show up, but I was so confused and afraid that just the sight of them made me scream in terror.

  I explored several different churches and religions, trying to understand life and find a place I could fit in. Nothing and nowhere felt right for me.

  I told my mother about seeing spirits and the fear and confusion I was experiencing. Because she, herself, had periodic encounters with spirits, she wasn't disturbed by the news. She shrugged my fear off and tried to comfort me by saying, "Don't be afraid. You have nothing to be afraid of. Only evil people need to be afraid."

Her words only compounded my fear. I thought, "I must be evil, since I am afraid." This caused me to become afraid of myself.

I felt trapped in a hopeless situation. I had no self-esteem. I felt broken and lost. I could not stand being me. I was shy and insecure and petrified that others would find out the truth of how unlovable and evil I feared that I was. The fear consumed me to the point that I was unable to go to bed at night unless my sister and our dog were sleeping in my room with me.

The Magic of Prayer and Tony

I continued to pray the best I could. Through constant prayer, I began to trust God. I began to trust that God wouldn't give me anything that I couldn't handle. Holding this truth in my heart and allowing myself to trust that everything in my life was happening for a reason I couldn't yet know, the fear began to subside. I began to feel peace and love in my heart. Little by little, I started to believe that I was actually a good person, and that everything that I had gone through was not punishment for being bad, after all.

One night, I discovered Tony Robbins on late night infomercials and started watching him. I loved his energy! He became my best friend, and I wished that I could meet him. I would watch his infomercials while doing my homework, as the rest of the house slept. It was my little piece of heaven. I imagined that I had his energy, his vitality, and his charisma. He became my role model, and I started practicing the tools he taught.

    Though still very shy and insecure, I became more energetic about my life. While my friends were dating, going to the movies, and having sleepovers, I was alone in my room learning as much as I could from Tony Robbins. He motivated me to start living instead of just existing. I began to feel happy. I began to enjoy my days in high school. I could hardly wait for each new day to begin. Though I still struggled with self-esteem issues, I allowed myself to become more outgoing. For the first time, I began attracting friends at school—REAL friends. And I met the boy who would later become my husband. By seventeen years old, I had completely changed my life from a prison of fear to a joyous life I could only have imagined a few years earlier.

    I continued praying and seeking God in my own way. My heart began to fill with light, and I slowly released my fears of the unseen. As my confidence and self-esteem grew, I became a peer mentor at school, so I could be a positive role model for students in grades nine and ten.

    I got involved in school activities and discovered I was very good at planning events. I loved organizing everything from bake sales to dances to fundraisers. I was able to move beyond my insecurities and express my enthusiastic school spirit. I didn't tell anyone about my past – my visions or my upbringing. I was no longer that former "me." I was a new person. And because of my involvement in school activities, I had a new life.

Releasing Fear

"I am willing to change and grow." — Louise L Hay

With high school behind me, I moved into adulthood. Though I had been able to free myself of many of my previous fears, I remained afraid of the dark. At twenty-three years old, I would run, with my eyes closed, to the light switch, and fumble around until I found it and could turn it on. I would not open my eyes until the lights were on. I was terrified of what I might see in the dark.

I was now a mother, and neither my husband nor I wanted our baby to be afraid of the dark. We knew that our baby would take on my debilitating fear if I didn't resolve it. I needed to find a way to be free of it as soon as possible, so he came up with a plan.

At that time, we lived on a farm. Together, we went into the barn and climbed up the ladder to the top level where the hay was stored. There was nothing here but rows and stacks of hay.

He took my hand and said, "I have an idea. If you agree to this, we can do it. I will turn the lights off, and I will stand right here, just five feet away from you. You will be safe, and you will not be alone. I am right here if you need me. Just reach for me, and I will be there. I want to show you that there is nothing to be afraid of. What do you think of when the lights are off?

There is nothing different, just look around you, there is only HAY. That's it. You do not need to worry, I am here for you," he said.

I was tired of the wild imaginings—the monsters and evil beings that I feared wanted to get me in the dark, so I agreed. I decided to challenge my fear. He asked if I was ready. I nodded. To someone on the ground floor, he shouted, "Turn off the lights!"

Standing in the barn, in the dark, surrounded by harmless hay, with my husband just a few feet away, I was overcome with the familiar terror. I began to shake and cry uncontrollably. I shrieked for the lights to be turned back on. Instead of the lights coming back on, my husband spoke. He asked me to look around, gently reassuring me there was no one there and that I was safe. Then he asked me the big question: "What are you thinking of?"

I screamed and demanded the lights to be turned back on. It had been less than three minutes, but it seemed like forever. My husband called for the lights to be turned back on. Once the lights were on, he asked again, "What were you thinking of when you were in the dark?"

Still shaking and crying, I answered, "That something evil is trying to get me! That I am not safe! That a monster is coming!"

He took me into his arms and reassured me that I was safe and that nothing evil was out there, trying to get me. He told me that I was just scaring myself with my imagination. He reassured me that he loved me and really wanted to help me be free.

That moment was a turning point for me. I heard the truth of his words, that it was my imagination that was scaring me, not anything outside of me. I realized he was right. I did not have to be afraid anymore.

I didn't know how to stop being afraid, so I turned to prayer. I asked God to help me – to guide me in the right direction – so I could be at peace and free from my fear. I didn't want my fear to prevent me from living life.

The next day, I realized, I was no longer afraid. I had received a miracle from God! I went about my day, and then realized, I had not experienced any fear that day. I tested it out with the dark. No fear! I was excited, surprised, and amazed! I had carried this fear for years, and it had seemed to grow stronger as time passed, yet in a day's time, it was completely gone! I felt like a new person. I was in awe. I knew that I had received a powerful miracle and that God had answered my prayers. Through my willingness to change, my willingness to see that I was the one who was creating the fear through my imagination, and my willingness to surrender the "how" of letting go of my fear, I had succeeded in healing myself of that fear. With the power of my mind and the grace of God, I was no longer afraid. God didn't "take" my fear away; instead I chose to let go of the fear. This was a powerful lesson to me about how much control I have in how I experience life. I can create fearful stories that limit my joy, or I can stop telling myself scary stories and allow my joy.

More Freedom

Through prayer, I had come to know that I was a part of God, and God was a part of me. Because of the barn experience, I now understood that as a part of God, I had power over things I had always believed I was a victim of. This made me want to learn more about the power we truly have, as individuals. I wanted to understand how I could affect and heal other problems I had. I wanted to break free of all my limitations. I wanted to love myself and stop running away from my God-given gifts. I wanted confidence, and I wanted to be able share the gift of freedom with others.

I constantly prayed about all of this, asking "Why am I here? What's my purpose? Why me? What's next?" I was so tired and frustrated of not knowing what I should do with my life that I gave God an ultimatum: (which I would not do now) "Okay, God. I know you love me, and I know I am here for a reason. If you don't show me the reason by tomorrow, then I am going to give up asking. I am not going to bother wondering what I am supposed to do with my life. I am just going to give up!"

Then I heard God whisper in my heart, "You are a healer. You are here to be of service to others."

I was shocked! Did I really just hear a voice? That was not mine? In my heart? Where did that voice come from? I am really a healer? How can I heal others if I need to be healed myself?

Turning to Google, I searched "being a healer," and I saw the word "Reiki." As I wondered what Reiki was, I heard that voice in my heart again: "Yes, Reiki is for you." (Reiki is energy healing and means "Universal Life Force Energy" in Japanese.)

Again, I was surprised. I had not expected an answer to my question, but maybe I should have. After all, I had asked for guidance. I had demanded that God show me my purpose.

I decided to trust this was truly a message from God and began searching for someone to teach me Reiki. My husband and I were planning to move back to the Toronto area, so I looked at several websites and contacted several Reiki masters in that area. No one responded. After several days of searching websites, reaching out, and getting no response, I became frustrated.

I prayed, "If I'm supposed to be a healer and do Reiki, why won't anyone write me back? If I don't find a teacher soon, then I'm giving up looking for one."

I started another search. The website I happened upon listed, at the bottom of the page, the name of someone in the same tiny rural community that I was living in. I decided to contact her. In no time, I received a response.

The woman and I arranged to meet for lunch to talk about Reiki and what I needed to do to get training. The way everything played out, made it seem as if had been divinely orchestrated. When I was focused on finding a teacher in a specific area, I kept hitting dead ends. When I let go of my expectations and opened to other possibilities, this woman fell right into my lap.

There was nothing that could have ever prepared me for what I experienced in the Reiki training. It was the polar opposite of what my life had been like as a child. The warm glow of Reiki enveloped me, as if I was being bathed in a pool of love. The depth of comfort and sense of belonging in the larger picture of life was indescribable. I knew, to the core of my being, that I was doing exactly what I had come into this world to do.

In addition to my daily prayers, I began meditating. My form of meditation was to focus on my breath and to feel appreciation. I also practiced using Reiki on myself. The more time I spent doing these things, the more at peace I felt. I began to see faint clouds of color around my hands, which I later learned was my aura, or personal energy field.

After 6 months, I moved to the next level of Reiki training. My teacher encouraged me to explore and embrace all of my spiritual gifts. She taught me to pay attention to signs and messages that were coming to me in numerous ways—through animals, timing of events, and more. I was amazed to see how many ways God could speak to me if I was willing to notice it. Messages were everywhere, all the time.

After completing the Reiki Master level of training, I began training in other forms of healing. I followed the doors, as they opened, and soon became a Certified Reflexologist and Certified Clinical Hypnotherapist. I was then guided to study metaphysical science, which led me to become an ordained minister.

As I learned and incorporated these tools into my own life, I slowly transformed. Like a caterpillar into a butterfly, my whole life changed—internally and externally.

As a teen, I had dreaded life. I could not imagine a future for myself other than the pain and sorrow I was living with. I was considered an "at risk" youth. Statistics predicted that I would not only stay trapped in this lifestyle, but that I would produce a new generation of the same dysfunction, pain, and sorrow. But I did not.

I overcame my past and created a new life for myself. I was a miracle! Not only did I change my life. With these tools, I was able to support others in creating changes in their lives, too. God was right! I was a healer! I had found my purpose!

Releasing More Fear

Though I had made great strides in my healing, I had many layers of fears to work through and heal. One was fear and judgment of Latinos.

My mother had married two times, each time to a Latino man. In her marriages, she had been cheated on and physically abused. This caused me to develop the belief that Latino men are not good. I am Latina, and my family is, too. Since most of the men in my family were also abusers or cheaters, they unknowingly reinforced this belief. I kept my belief hidden, because I knew how everyone would react if they knew. Deep inside I was afraid of Latinos, and I didn't want to get close to anyone Latino.

During my hypnosis training, my teacher asked the class, "Who would like to come up here and demonstrate for the class how to let go of a fear?"

Even though I was still a little shy, I recognized that I needed help letting go of the negative attitudes I had towards Latinos. I volunteered for the demonstration.

My teacher asked me question after question, and I started crying in front of the class. I was embarrassed and ashamed to admit that I judged Latinos. At the same time, I also felt waves of relief wash over me. Hiding my judgment had weighed heavily on me, as I fought to pretend it didn't exist. I was finally able to admit this belief and examine it closely.

My teacher asked questions like, "Why are you afraid of Latinos?" "Can you think of a Latino that isn't mean?" "How does this fear serve you?" "Do you want to release this fear?"

I shared with the class about my stepfather, the pain I watched my mother go through, and the fear and pain I had experienced. I was honest with myself about how, despite my experiences, this belief and judgment was taking a negative toll on me, and that I truly did want to be free of it.

Using hypnosis, my teacher took me on a journey to "cut cords." "Cutting cords" is a powerful tool of hypnosis to free someone of negativity related to people or events in your life. As she guided me through the visualization, I was able to see things from a new perspective. I saw that I had given all Latinos the face of my stepfather. I had made him their representative, in all of his dysfunction. I was now able to separate my stepfather and his actions from Latinos, as a whole. I was able to see that everything that had happened had a higher purpose, and that I was free to let go of the pain I had attached to the events, if I wanted to.

I chose to let the pain go. The "cords" that connected me to the people and events that had formed my negative beliefs about Latinos were severed. I was free!

After the session, I could tell that my feelings towards Latinos had changed. I felt a new openness toward Latinos that I had never felt before.

Everyone in the class could tell a shift had taken place. It was a tremendous healing experience for me. What my class did, was hold space for me. Holding space is a sacred skill; you allow others to release their emotions in a sacred and safe environment. Without judgments or giving any advice. Giving voice to my fears in front of everyone was a huge release for me. Sometimes holding space is the best way to help others.

I am...Empowered!

Because of my past, my low self-esteem limited me in almost every area of my life. I had no confidence in myself, which prevented me from speaking in front of even small groups. And that was just the tip of the iceberg! Over time, I was able to release my self-esteem issues using the tools of hypnosis, Reiki, and affirmations.

I was introduced to Louise L Hay's book You Can Heal Your Life and decided to do just that—heal my life! I knew that I had two choices – I could remain the child with low self-esteem and lots of fears living in an adult body, or I could heal my life and become an empowered woman, embracing my light.

Louise is an avid proponent of mirror work and affirmations. Having learned about her childhood and how her life had unfolded into who she was, now, I was motivated to see what magic this would work in me. I wanted to love myself the way she loved herself.

Every morning, using a mirror, I looked myself in the eye. I said kind and loving things to myself over and over. Everything I needed to hear and know about myself as a child, I said to myself: "You are divine." "You are beautiful." "You are loveable exactly as you are." "You are safe."

It was difficult in the beginning, because my wounded inner child argued with me. She was not beautiful. She was not loveable. And so on. I had to be patient with myself. Knowing that my inner child believed all the negative and painful messages she had been given during my first six years, I knew it would take some work to change those negative programs into positive programs. But I was worth it!

Every day, I repeated kind and loving words to myself in the mirror. Slowly, I began to see changes. There was no more resistance to the kind words, no more internal arguments for my less-than-ness. I began to see the real beauty inside myself. I started to see my truth, my light. I realized I had to be full of self-love before I could truly accept and give love.

My affirmations became first person: "I am beautiful." "I am loveable." "I am kind and loving to everyone I meet." "I am open to receive all the miracles and magic God wants to give me." Because I was able to change my negative childhood programming and transform my life, I know that anyone can. Anyone can use affirmations to transform negative, disempowering beliefs into positive, empowering ones.

The Light Within

"All the darkness in the world cannot extinguish the light of a single candle." — *St. Francis of Assisi*

When we consciously connect with Source, we radiate love and light, and there is no reason to fear. As I embraced my light, I was able to release my fear. I could not hold onto both at the same time.

A teacher once told me: "Imagine having two rooms, side-by-side. One room is full of light, while the other room is full of darkness. Now imagine that there is a wall separating these rooms. On that wall, there is a tiny hole. The hole is the size of a pencil tip. No matter how small the hole is light will always shine through. The light will shine through the wall, into the room of darkness. You will always see a ray of light in the room full of darkness. You will never see a ray of darkness in the room full of light. It's impossible. Darkness cannot exist in the light. Only light can exist in light."

This analogy helped me accept the truth that darkness can't overpower light. The power of darkness is only an illusion. When we are connected to Source, the Divine Light, nothing is more powerful. There is nothing to fear.

Knowing that I am a child of this Light allows me to release my fears and trust that no harm is going to ever come to me or my family, and that anything that appears to be harm— such as what I experienced as a child—is really only a temporary experience that will reveal its purpose at a later time.

Struggles are Blessings

As I continued my journey of healing, I learned the importance of forgiving. We often think that when we forgive someone, we are letting them off the hook, or somehow declaring that what was done to us wasn't that bad or wasn't a big deal.

That is not what forgiveness is at all. The word forgive means "to release the desire or power to punish." Forgiveness is all about setting ourselves free.

When we hold resentment, we want the other person to be punished in some way. Usually, there is no way for them to receive the punishment we feel they deserve, and even if someone does receive punishment, we rarely feel any relief. The punishment will not relieve our pain, because the punishment has nothing to do with us.

Likewise, our forgiveness will not let the other person off the hook, because our forgiveness has nothing to do with the other person. When we forgive, we are releasing the desire to punish the other person. Forgiveness unhooks us from the negative aspects of the experience. It lets us walk away from the pain instead of dragging it around with us the rest of our lives. It allows us to start healing the wound that was inflicted on us.

When we hold onto our resentments, we carry those people and painful memories around with us, not just in our minds, but also in the cells of our bodies. The pain, the anger, the hatred, the self-pity, and the sense of powerlessness are all toxic chemicals that have been, and still are, stored in our bodies. The longer we hold onto the resentment, the longer we slowly poison our cells. Each time we recall a past event and feel the old familiar emotion from it, we are giving ourselves another dose of poison.

When we are able to forgive others, we release these toxic chemicals from our cells and bodies and can improve our health, both physically and mentally.

Anger and resentment can also blind us to the gifts that negative experiences usually carry. Forgiveness can open our eyes to those hidden gifts. As I began to forgive those who had hurt me in my past, I began to also see the gifts that each of them had given me. I came to the realization that my childhood had actually been a blessing. I understood that I needed to experience each of those struggles and all of that pain in order to become the person I am today.

I forgave my father for walking out on us and not being there for me. I forgave my stepfather for his abuse. I realized that he, as a product of abuse by his father, was acting out his own pain and was parenting the only way he knew how. He showed me the kind of husband and father I did not want to have and helped me clarify the kind of relationship I wanted to have in the future. Through him, I learned that instead of feeling like a victim and cowering in fear, I can access my courage, speak up, and take action when I need to.

I forgave the kids who bullied me during my school years. I can see that these children gave me the opportunity to experience powerless victimhood so that I could find my power and springboard into the strong goddess that I am today. Experiencing the bullying also allows me to empathize with bullying victims and empower them to find and reclaim their power.

In retrospect, I can see that each of these experiences helped me learn and grow. I know I am stronger and wiser because of them. This perspective makes me appreciate them and the struggles they provided me. I can see that each of my abusers showed up in my life to teach me something. Each of them contributed to me. Each made me stronger. Each had a hand in making me into who I am today. How can I hold a grudge against a teacher?

I needed to learn how to love myself, to embrace my gifts, and to trust in the Higher Power. In order to truly learn what Love is I needed to experience its opposite. Despite what statistics predicted, I was able to break the cycle of generational poverty and abuse. I have demonstrated that someone who comes from the projects or from an abusive home is not destined to be an abuser or with an abuser. I have shown that it is possible to make huge changes to your life by following your inner guidance and making baby-step changes along the way. I was able to overcome my barriers and limitations. So can you!

PART III

DESERVING

"As you become more clear about who you really are, you'll be better able to decide what is best for you – the first time around."

- Oprah Winfrey

In both my private life and professional life, I encounter a lot of women who feel unworthy and undeserving. They give their power away to their spouses, bosses, friends, and even strangers. You need to believe that you deserve the best in life for the best to come to you.

Once, I wrote in a friend's birthday card: "Happy Birthday! Wishing you lots of love and happiness, and I hope you receive everything you deserve." My friend was offended. She said, "Everything I deserve? That sounds bad!"

My friend was in a difficult relationship and gave her power away to her husband on a daily basis. Because she was in an unhappy place, she felt she deserved to feel unhappy. On some level, she believed she didn't deserve love, happiness, and goodness, but rather the opposite, and that was exactly what she was experiencing! I assured her that I was saying she deserves love and happiness. I was coming from a place of love, wishing her more love, because I knew she truly deserved love. After telling her we all deserve the best in life, and she is worthy of love, then she understood what I meant.

We all are worthy of love, happiness, and abundance in all areas of our lives. We have to learn to accept the kindness, the acts of service and the love that comes our way. We all deserve love. Love is our truth. Love will set us free and fill our lives with happiness.

When we make the conscious effort to choose love, no matter what, we will begin to believe and accept that we are worthy of the best! We will begin to believe and accept that we deserve happiness! We will begin to believe and accept that it's perfectly fine to ask for help when we need it. We will begin to believe and accept that we can achieve anything we desire!

If we desire to be happy, we must believe we are worthy of happiness. If we do not believe this, we will unconsciously sabotage ourselves and deprive ourselves of happiness. We deserve the best in life, no matter what we have been told by others. If we don't believe this, we will unconsciously ensure that we do not get the best. For us to truly be open to receive all of

God's gifts and the abundance God intends to flow into our lives, we need to challenge the false belief of unworthiness and replace it with a belief and knowing that we are worthy!

We have to train ourselves to feel worthy of love so we can truly receive love. We have established habits that cause us to deflect love by default, and argue with the love and goodness that tries to come to us. Because of our beliefs in unworthiness, we refuse and deflect love, and then wonder why we are so unhappy. We have the power to change that!

A first step to embracing our True Selves is setting aside some time to focus on ourselves. At first, this will seem selfish, and others may be quick to point this out, but have a closer look. First, if you're on an airplane and the pressure changes, making the oxygen masks drop out of the ceiling, what are you supposed to do? Take care of you first, and then help those beside you. Is that being selfish? No! It is taking steps that are necessary to ensure that you can be of service to others. Second, why would someone want you to put them ahead of you and your own needs?

As you spend time with yourself, you may discover you have supportive beliefs, as well as sabotaging beliefs, about yourself. This is gold! Supportive beliefs can be used as leverage as you begin to challenge them and change the negative beliefs you hold. As we begin to change our beliefs and accept that we are worthy of happiness and that we deserve the best in life, we can be open to receive all the abundance that is constantly flowing into our lives.

Saint Peter

Be authentic with yourself. Feel your worthiness. Remember you are made from Divine Love and light, and we are one with Source. If we are one with Source, that means there are miracles and blessings that we are entitled to. These miracles and blessings ought to be more commonplace than we let them be, because they are from the same Source as we are. When we open to the truth of who we are, we can allow these miracles and blessings to flow into our lives and live the lives we intended.

Cheryl Richardson tells a story that illustrates the importance of asking for miracles and blessings, staying open to receive them, and believing that we are worthy of receiving them:

"A man dies and arrives in heaven. Saint Peter greets him at the Pearly Gates and welcomes him in. Saint Peter begins giving the man a tour of heaven. Everything is magical, peaceful, and more beautiful than he could have imagined – beautiful colors, beautiful landscapes, and beautiful buildings. They enter a building beaming with light. The building was a library of sorts, full of rows and rows of gold filing cabinets. Saint Peter explained that each soul had its own cabinet, and the man was invited to review his if he wished. The man was curious and eagerly accepted the invitation. They arrived at the file cabinet with the man's name on it. Saint Peter nodded for him to open his cabinet, and as he did, stars – glistening and beaming with light

– spilled out from the cabinet. The man asked, "What is this?" Saint Peter answered, "These are all the blessings and miracles that were yours but you never asked for."

When I first heard that story, I got chills over my whole body, which to me is confirmation that this is truth, and I must listen and apply this to my life. Every night after this, when I prayed at bedtime with my children, we added, "God, please give me all the blessings and miracles that I am entitled to. Thank you."

Each of us deserves blessings, miracles, happiness, joy and love. Maybe there really is a cabinet full of glistening, beautiful, star-like blessings and miracles just waiting to make some magic in our lives. It would be awful to find out they were available and the only reason we didn't get to experience them was because we didn't ask. Start asking for your blessings and miracles now, and be open to receive them.

Once you start connecting daily with your Spirit and becoming aware of your blessings in life, your life will begin to flow with more grace and peace. You will start noticing all the blessings and "glistening stars" flowing into your life like magic.

Notice them, acknowledge them, and appreciate them. Through eyes of gratitude, everything can become a blessing. Every event, big or small, can be a reminder of things to be grateful for. Every day, be on the lookout for blessings coming into your life. Start seeing everything as a blessing. Trust that life will only bring to you things that are going to benefit you in some way, even if it looks like a disaster. It may be difficult at first, but with practice, it will become second nature to wake up with gratitude and go to sleep with gratitude.

Balance – It's Necessary and You Deserve It

We have been taught that it is selfish to look after our own needs, and that we need to put others first. This puts us on an unhealthy track. If we constantly give and give – to work, family, friends, school – without giving to ourselves, we become like a table with one leg too short. You've probably sat at one of those tables at a coffee shop or somewhere. Looking at the table, it appears perfectly fine. Once you place your items on the table and sit down, it becomes obvious the table is not balanced. The unbalanced table can range from frustrating to dangerous, depending on what you've placed on the table (some coffee shops heat their water to over 200°!). It is the same with us. When we are out of balance, our lives can become anything from frustrating to dangerous; depending on how long we neglect ourselves and our own needs.

Our lives have many demands, and it's important that we find balance. In my life, I have to find balance in my many roles: nurturing mother, good friend, amazing lover, loving sister and daughter, wise teacher, centered holistic practitioner, and enthusiastic minister. As I give of myself to others, I must also make time to give to myself. Without it, I would be out of balance and it would be easy to become resentful of my roles. My service to others would feel more like those I'm serving are taking from me instead of me giving to them.

It is imperative that we take time each day to do things that fill our love tanks. We must do things that make us feel good, balanced, and loved. You are worthy of that good feeling, and if you do not take care of your love tank, then you will be running on empty. If you don't give to yourself, then you will have nothing to give others.

Each of us needs different things to find balance. One way I fill my love tank is by attending uplifting events. These kinds of events are like nectar for my soul – refreshing and nourishing. They invigorate, refresh, and renew me.

There are people in my life that cannot understand why I attend them, especially since I am a metaphysical teacher, myself. They think I am weird for even having the philosophies that I do, never mind spending time away from my family to learn more.

I tell them, "Everyone is different. Some people enjoy watching soap operas. Some people play golf or go to the bar. I enjoy going to positive and empowering seminars. I treat myself to an event once or twice a year to network, learn, and grow. It is one way I nurture myself and fill my love tank. It makes me feel good, and I am not hurting anyone, so why do you mind?"

They just roll their eyes and let me be. I understand that they are not on the same path as I am, and they can't see things in the same way I do. I know they are doing the best they can and are trying to find happiness in their own ways. I can gently allow them to not understand me and my choices without trying to convince them, argue with them, or make them wrong in any way. Their ways are not my ways, and I allow them to do what they feel they need to do in order to fill their own love tanks.

The bottom line is: you must do what feels good for you. Don't measure yourself against others, or do what others think you should do to find balance. We each must find our own way to bring ourselves into balance.

Some people fill their love tanks through art, music, dance, or taking classes. There are as many ways to fill your tank, as there are people. It's important that you find whatever feels right for you. Love and respect yourself enough to make time for you. You deserve it!

In my circle of friends, I am known as the "always positive, full of energy, super-mom," – their words, not mine. My friends often ask me, "How do you manage with four kids? How do you stay calm, have time to work out, get dressed up, work, write a book, and still have the energy for near-daily sex too?!"

My answer to them is always, "You must find balance. Take time each day for yourself. You deserve it. You need it. Do something that makes you happy."

I love working out, so I workout. I love being happy, so I spread happiness. I love playing with my kids, spending time with my husband – so I make time for them. I make sure I make time for everything I love. I make time for myself each day, even if it's just 1 hour a day to read a good book, go for a walk, workout, and just be alone, unplugged from everything. I balance my time, so I can be the best version of myself in every situation.

When my husband comes home from work, after our family dinner and the "Roses and Thrones" are done, if I haven't had a chance to work out or get alone time, I go out and take one hour to be alone. I may meditate, go for a walk in nature, go work out, or just spend time alone.

It is not unusual for me to get a phone call at 8:00 pm or later from someone who is emotional or needs a shoulder to cry on. I do not mind because I love assisting others. My husband knows and accepts that this is part of who I am and how I honor myself. If I am out for 2-4 hours with a friend one night, then I make sure the next night I am unplugged from social media/phone and cuddling with my husband.

I enjoy going out and helping my friends. I enjoy playing and reading books to my children. And each night, afterwards, I enjoy spending time with my husband. All of this together is how I create balance for myself.

It is important that you do things that you enjoy, that resonate with you. Find your thing and do it!

NO = "New Opportunities"

Many of us have been infected with the Disease to Please. It began in childhood. When we did the "right" thing, and we were rewarded with a smile, praise, or maybe even a treat. When we did the "wrong" thing, we were penalized with a frown, reprimand, or maybe even a spanking. We learned quickly that our lives seemed to work better if we made those around us happy, through our words, deeds, or behaviors. We learned that others' moods – good and bad – were because of us. We learned we were responsible for the others' feelings.

All these years later, we still carry that false burden. We still believe it is our "job" to make sure those around us are happy, especially our families – our spouses, children, parents, siblings, etc. We often ignore our own needs and neglect our own feelings, because we learned that our needs and feelings were not as important as those around us. When we cater to those around us in this way, we get locked into this role, repeating this behavior, with no easy way out. Others' get accustomed to being number one, and we find it increasingly difficult to break the pattern.

"No," isn't hard to say. It's a quick and easy word. It rolls easily off the tongue of every 2-year old, yet we find it difficult to say because we have learned to attach guilt to "no." The association of guilt with "no" is what makes us feel we cannot say it to others; especially to those we love and care about. We must learn to say "no" without feeling guilt.

We are entitled to make our own decisions. The choices we make are our choices to make. When someone asks us to do something, the request presents us with a choice – "yes" or "no." Often, obligation makes us feel we have to say "yes," and guilt lingers with "no," but we do not need to feel obligated to do something just because we are asked to do it, or feel guilty about saying "no." We have a choice, every time.

Sometimes we may feel we have no choice, but really, we do. We have learned that others may try to get us to feel guilty for saying "no." It is important to remember that this attempt to "guilt" us into a "yes" is just a form of manipulation; a mind game that the ego likes to play.

If our "no" is met with a "why," it is an indicator that we are about to encounter a manipulation attempt. Most people, in this situation, do not ask "why" as a way to understand us and our reasoning, but rather as a way to assess our reasoning in order to re-present their request in a way that they can activate our guilt so they can get their way.

Sometimes people feel they need to explain everything in detail when answering "no." The other party may not even have to ask "why," because our own guilt at being "selfish" makes us feel we need to explain "why" in order to justify it to ourselves.

We do not owe anyone any kind of explanation. A "no" doesn't need to be justified. It needs no explanation. "No" is a complete answer. An honest and truthful "no" is enough.

Saying "no" when we mean "no" is not selfish. It is important to say "no" when we mean "no" in order to honor ourselves and to have balance in our lives.

Saying "no" creates a space for New Opportunities to enter into our lives – New Opportunities for all the blessings and miracles that we are entitled to! "No" is a positive statement that allows us to have a New Opportunity to follow our hearts, be true to ourselves, and feel happy. Saying "no" gives us an opportunity to be honest with ourselves, to show love to ourselves, to respect ourselves, and to be in integrity with ourselves. Being honest with ourselves and coming from a place of self-awareness and authenticity will also communicate to others that we are strong, present, and listen to our hearts.

When we say "no" and honor our feelings, we will find that other opportunities will begin to present for us, because we will be in alignment with Source. As we say "no" to things that we don't really want to do, we begin to raise our vibrations as we clear out the vibrations of obligation and resentment. As we honor our feelings and come into alignment with our truth, New Opportunities that resonate with our new, higher vibration will begin to present.

Making the transition from People Pleaser to Authentic Ally can be difficult. We have had years of people pleasing experience, and old habits die-hard. Baby steps, one moment at a time, is the way to make this change. Observing our actions without judgment and internally committing, again and again, to do it differently next time is more productive than berating ourselves for doing what we've always done.

When asked to do something, if the first feeling is uncertainty, it is helpful to respond with something like, "I need to sit with this for a while, and I will get back to you." Instead of agreeing to do something and then regretting that we agreed, this response allows us the chance to check within and formulate and deliver an authentic response.

Taking a moment to sit with what presents is a good tool to use to prevent knee-jerk reactions. Often we react too fast and agree to something without truly wanting to agree, simply because we want to please others.

Practice checking in with yourself. When someone asks you to do something, take a moment to notice what feelings you experience? Do you feel joy? Frustration? Love? Guilt? Listen to your feelings and say "no" when you feel any unpleasant feeling about the request. It doesn't have to make sense to you or anyone else, and no one has to understand or agree with your decision. Just trust yourself and your feelings.

I used to be a chronic people pleaser. I found it almost impossible to say "no" to people and often felt taken advantage of by others. I used to agree to do things for other people because I didn't want to disappoint them. I found myself agreeing to do things that I didn't want to do – from doing a friend's homework in high school, to agreeing to host a party in adulthood, or even to baby-sit.

My inability to say "no" was causing me to feel like a doormat, and I was becoming resentful. I knew this would slowly kill these relationships. I had to learn how to say "no."

In the beginning, it was very difficult to say "no," because I felt responsible and obligated to make others' happy. When I said, "no," I felt guilty. I felt like I was selfish and wasn't a "good" person. Some people let me know that they, too, thought I was being selfish and accused me of not caring about them or their feelings. Ironically, it was because I cared about their feelings that I had gotten myself into the people-pleasing bind that I was now trying to escape.

My spiritual journey was teaching me that it was important that I honor my true feelings, and I realized that I needed to teach myself how to feel comfortable with the word "no." When someone asked me to do something, I needed to take a moment and check with myself before I gave my answer. If I didn't want to do something, I had to honor that and say, "no," and stick to my "no," no matter how "disappointed" the other person was, or how badly they "needed" me, or whatever other argument they offered in order to pressure me into changing my "no" to a "yes."

It didn't happen quickly. It took an enormous amount of practice. Sometimes I was successful with saying, and sticking to, "no," sometimes I let guilt turn my "no" into an "oh, alright," and sometimes I'd forget and revert to my knee-jerk reaction of saying "yes" without thinking.

As I got better at saying "no" and meaning it, I learned that saying "no" gave me freedom to say a resentment-free "yes" to things that I didn't mind doing. At the same time, this made my "yes" have more value than it had ever had before. No longer did people assume that I would do anything that was asked of me. My "yes" became appreciated by others instead of taken for granted. What a wonderful gift I had given myself!

Instead of "no" being a negative, guilt-inducing word, "NO" came to mean "New Opportunities" for me – opportunities to honor myself, opportunities for others to respect me and my boundaries, opportunities for me to respect myself and trust myself to be sensitive to my own needs, and opportunities to bless others with my authentic "yes." It also meant "New Opportunities" in the sense that if I said "no" to this request; I would be able to say, "yes" to something that I truly did want to do when it presented.

Today, if someone calls me and "needs" something, if I am tired, have had a long day, or simply don't feel like that is how I want to spend my time, I honor myself and politely say "no." I have learned that I must love myself enough to respect my true feelings. When I do that, I teach others that they can count on me to be honest with them about my feelings. They can trust that we will never have an undercurrent of resentment in our relationship, because I will never feel taken advantage of.

Affirmations that have helped me release guilt:

"I honor myself, and let go of guilt. I am worthy of being honest with myself. Others deserve my honesty. Saying what I feel is easy. Saying "no" is easy. I release any guilt from my being. I embrace the love that I am."

Saying no doesn't have to make us feel bad. It can be liberating. True liberation happens when we can stand in our truth, follow our hearts, and stop worrying about what others will think of us.

We have the right to shine the beautiful light that we are. We can live our own self-determined life story instead of letting others create it for us through obligation and guilt.

YES = "You Embracing Source"

In an orchestra, musicians focus on the part they each play in the larger picture. They are each in the present moment, fully focused on following the flow of the conductor's guidance – all in unity, all as one, producing a musical masterpiece. The timing is perfect, the instruments complement each other, and the result is an unfolding of musical perfection that astounds the audience.

Source is like the conductor of an orchestra, and each of us is a single musician. We each have our individual contribution to the whole, yet we cannot see the whole picture the way the conductor can.

When we are in the present moment and focus on following our guidance, our lives become a masterpiece. Everything unfolds at the exact right time. People come and go at just the right time. Things we need come into our lives, and things that no longer serve us leave our lives – all at the exact right time. The timing is perfect and everything complements everything else. It is utter perfection!

When we embrace Source, anything is possible, and our lives become more than we could have imagined. When we are honest with ourselves and honor our hearts and our inner guidance, we connect to, and flow with, the infinite power of God. We can say "yes" to the flow of life, no matter what presents. When we say "yes" to life, we each create our own masterpiece. We open to receive all of God's blessings and miracles.

We are one with Source, and by saying "yes" to Source, we embrace ourselves fully and accept ourselves for who and where we are right now; without comparing ourselves to others or judging things as different from what they "should" be. Saying "yes" is embracing all aspects of ourselves, treating ourselves with kindness, and going with the flow of our divine natures.

We deserve to say "yes" to life and to let go of fear, shame, and judgments. When we start to embrace Source, we start to remember who we really are. We are meant to be exactly whom and where we are. There are no accidents. Our presence is a miracle.

Embracing Source is akin to thanking God for creating us just the way we are –perfect beings! We are perfect in the eyes of God, and that's all that really matters. Embracing Source gives us the power to be authentic and to live our lives with unconditional love. It allows us to accept all the things that come our way with grace and to see everything in life as a blessing.

When we are open and embracing Source, we begin to see divine connections in our everyday moments. We begin to notice divine interventions, synchronicities, blessings, and lessons along our journeys.

Living Like a Squirrel

Like a squirrel gathering nuts to store for the winter, we can gather a storehouse of tools and knowledge and be constantly open to more growth. What we are ready to learn will show up exactly when we are ready to learn it. As the saying goes, "When the student is ready, the teacher will appear."

As we build on the knowledge and skills that we have, we have more tools to access. The accumulation of these tools combined with our connection to Source allows us to be a conduit of love and healing for others at unexpected moments. It also can be a source of healing for ourselves.

In my own life, I had fear about things unseen. As I began exploring and learning, I began to heal my fears. I learned about crystal healing, pendulums, tarot, the chakras, auras, Reiki, hypnosis, past lives, the law of attraction, and metaphysical science. I learned about Source and how to access my gifts. I stayed open to the flow of the divine and decided to let go of fear and to never let it hold me back.   And I continue to learn even today.

I am like a squirrel, gathering "nuts" – gathering many different tools of wisdom and using them in divine timing. I collect valuable information and teachings and store these treasures until the time they are needed, remembering what I've learned and applying the knowledge when it is needed. By taking action and applying our knowledge, we continue to heal and grow.

Squirrels also illustrate to us the importance of having balance. They work hard preparing for the future, and they play hard, too, leaping from branch to branch and running free. The squirrel can be a reminder to create balance in life, because we deserve to feel satisfied in all areas of our lives.

PART IV

DIVINE

"Take the first step in faith. You don't have to see the whole staircase; just take the first step."   -   *Martin Luther King Jr.*

I believe, with all my heart, that we are each part of the Divine Source. I believe that we are all capable of receiving divine messages, encounters, and blessings on a daily basis. When we practice conscious awareness of the Divine's presence in everything around us, we start to recognize the magic and miracles that are in our lives.

There is an abundance of blessings available to us. Many of us are closed to them, as we scramble around in our hustle-bustle lives. As we go about our day-to-day business, we tend to take things for granted. We expect things to be the way they were yesterday: the sun rises, the electricity works, our hearts beat, the car starts, the water in the tap is clean, and our loved ones are alive. We get in routines and forget how special and miraculous these mundane things truly are.

When we take a moment to notice and appreciate these things, we increase our connection to the Divine and to each other. By taking even just five minutes in the morning to notice these blessings, we set our minds up to notice more of them throughout the day. At the same time, we energetically extend an invitation for more blessings to come our way, in all forms.

These gifts and blessing are not exclusive. They are available to each of us. We only need to be open to receive them. In this chapter, I share some of my personal experiences of Divine interventions, magic, and miracles. I know you have had Divine experiences, as well. As you read about my experiences, be open to recall yours. You may have had experiences that you may not have realized were Divine. Allow yourself to see them through new eyes and become aware of the Divine happenings that have taken place. Be on the lookout for them in your day-to- day life. You are surrounded by Divine Love that is always conspiring for your highest good.

Manifesting My Future Husband

When I was 15 years old, in high school, some Latino guys made it very clear they were interested in me. They would flirt with me and ask me out. I was shy and scared and didn't like the attention. I politely declined their offers, but they were not dissuaded.

One day, one of them challenged my rejection and said, "Come on. Just go out with me. You need to practice kissing before you get married. Stop being such a goody two-shoes. You can lie to your mom, you know. She doesn't have to find out if you have a boyfriend."

I was tired of hearing him tell me I should date, so without thinking, I blurted out the first thing that popped into my mind. "Actually, I have a boyfriend, already." I said. It wasn't true, so I was surprised when I said it.

He didn't believe me and said, "Oh, yeah, right! Then what school does he go to?"

"He goes to St. Kitts," I answered, again speaking what had just popped into my mind.

The Latino guys laughed. "St. Kitts? That's not a school! That's a Caribbean island!"

I had no idea that St. Kitts was an island, but I quickly covered, and said, "I meant that he is from St. Kitts, but he goes to St. Pat's. All these Saints get me confused."

Still not buying my story, he asked, "What does he look like, then?"

I knew they weren't falling for it. I kept going anyway.

"He is tall, black, and has green eyes," I said.

I could tell they knew I was lying. I could see it in their smirks.

For three months, the guys made fun of me, saying: "Say hello to your imaginary boyfriend from St. Kitts!"

They laughed at me, but I didn't care. I was relieved, because they had finally stopped pestering me to go on dates with them.

Two years passed, and I forgot about this incident. A new student arrived in my school. He was a tall, black guy with mesmerizing, green eyes. We became friends and eventually started dating. I was seventeen-years old and had never been kissed. He was my very first boyfriend.

We dated for three months before I asked him where his family was from. His beautiful features did not suggest a particular ethnic heritage, and I was curious.

"St. Kitts," he said.

The episode with the Latino guys from two years earlier flashed into my mind. I was astonished! I had predicted the love of my life! I was in awe, and I knew he was my soul mate. I knew that I had received a Divine message two years earlier, when I was only 15-years old!

Manifesting in real life the exact guy I had described 2 years earlier made me realize that there was more to life than meets the eye. I was intrigued with what else was "out there" that I could tap into to design my life. I prayed for more clarity and understanding of this experience.

Rowan was a gift from the Universe, in more than just the sense of being my life-mate. Rowan was also my awakening. I was amazed by this premonition and knew that it had been a message from the Divine Source. I knew that I had had this experience for a reason, and I wanted to understand how it had happened. I had the sense that this experience somehow connected to my ability to see spirits. Both were gifts that no one I knew talked about, but both were clearly real. I decided then that I would do whatever it took to let go of the fear I had learned from my religious upbringing. I decided to stop searching for labels to describe or define what I believed.

I knew my fears were holding me back in life, and the only way to release them was to face and embrace them. I decided to embrace my fear of the unknown and began exploring other teachings.

I remembered seeing a renowned psychic on a TV talk show and how excited I had felt as I listened to her speak. She had talked about spirits and receiving messages, and I remembered how much better I felt knowing that someone else was having experiences similar to mine. As she spoke, there was no hint of fear in her voice or any suggestion of her ability being evil or the least bit worrisome. She openly embraced her gifts and used them to help others. It made me feel good knowing that others were also getting information from the Divine, and they were not afraid.

I found one of the psychic's books and began reading it. The more I read, the more I discovered how alike we were. I resonated with some of her teachings, as she put words to what I was experiencing and had come to believe through my experiences. Using this book, I began to trust my intuition and worked to further develop it.

This particular psychic believed that we choose our experiences before we are born into this lifetime. This idea helped me find peace with the painful childhood I had experienced. I thought, "If I chose my childhood to be the way it was, I must have done it to make me a stronger person, spiritually, and to learn to have faith in God."

If I had planned a difficult childhood, it made sense that I would have planned to have these abilities to help me along my journey.

I also liked the idea that perhaps this ability had been given to me so that I could help others in a unique way, just as this psychic was. I started experimenting with my gifts. At small parties or other get-togethers, I gave little readings. While holding a person's hand, I felt the energy; saw images, and shared the information I had received. I didn't read the lines on their palms; instead, I translated the energy.

As I released my fears and relaxed into my gifts, I was able to slowly embrace this part of myself. My gifts became stronger and I developed new abilities.

I learned about auras and gazing with unfocused eyes, gently observing the area outside someone or something and began practicing on my friends. As I did, I began to see a faint glow of color around them. The more I practiced, the more easily I could see it. As I practiced even more, I started seeing aura's everywhere—around the trees, my friends, my family, and inanimate objects.

When I first started gazing, I could only see the energy if there was a light background behind the person I was gazing. With practice, it became so easy that I could just ask myself, "What color is the aura?" and the color would pop right up.

As this happened, I remembered that as a child, I would see a glow of light around the trees when I was hiking with my family. I loved it when my mom and I would drive somewhere at night, because I enjoyed seeing the glow of colored light around the stores in the distance and the light posts and the little particles in the air right in front of me. I didn't know that I was seeing the energy and aura of these objects, and I didn't know others couldn't see this. I thought everyone could see what I was seeing. When I learned they couldn't, it made me feel like there was something wrong with me. Developing this fear closed down my ability, and when the lights disappeared, I felt normal again.

As I reawakened my ability to see energy, I realized that I had had this gift from a young age and just didn't understand what it was at the time. I had no one who could relate to it and explain to me what was happening and that it wasn't just normal, but that it was a blessing and a gift! What I was doing was reacquainting myself with my gifts and learning ways to by-pass the blocks that my fear had put in place to "protect" me.

I practiced every day, knowing that because my intention was pure, my gifts would bless others as I developed them. As I became more comfortable with my abilities, my fear lessened and I experienced more synchronicities, and I received more and more messages that I was on the right path.

Angels Saved My Life!

I believe in angels. I always have. I believe that guardian angels are watching over each one of us and can assist us anytime we ask them to. Some people are more aware of their presence than others. Some can feel their warmth or talk to them each day like close friends. Some may see a feather along their path and recognize it as a reminder that they are not alone. Some even hear their angels speak directly to them.

I remember the first time I heard my angels speak to me – July 9, 2003. My young family and I had recently moved from Toronto to live in the country with my mother, near Niagara Falls, Ontario. I wanted to pursue my gifts and use them to help others. My extended family members didn't support me in my vision. They knew I had a completed post-secondary training for a career in the Tourism and Hospitality industry and constantly pushed me to get a job in my field of training. They also disapproved of me having a child at such a young age and felt I was taking advantage of my mother by moving in with her. There was a lot of pressure for me to stop thinking "foolishly" and to get a "real" job.

In order to get them off my back, I got a job as a Reservations Agent at a hotel in Niagara Falls. I had been at the job for a month and could not stand it. I hated answering phone calls from the basement of the hotel, hidden away from the rest of the world. I felt like I had "sold out" by taking a job that did not nurture my soul. I soothed myself by telling myself that with this income, I could continue my Reiki training and be able to study other things, such as crystal healing, reflexology, and hypnosis, and eventually make my dream a reality.

At midnight, my shift finally ended. As I walked to my van, I had a thought: "It's a good thing I am driving a van. If I get into an accident, I won't get hurt."

I didn't like driving late at night, and with a 45-minute drive home ahead of me, in the country with no street lights and no cell phone, it brought me a degree of comfort. Little did I know that this thought was my intuition preparing me for what was about to happen.

About 5 minutes outside the city, I turned onto a dark, narrow, 2-lane road and headed into the country. I was going 100 kilometers per hour, listening to music, and looking forward to climbing into bed. Suddenly, I felt warmth surround me, and I heard a voice: "Slow down. You might get into an accident." The voice was so loud and clear that it sounded like someone was in the van with me.

Chills ran through my body. I turned off my music, and thought, "Maybe the angels are warning me. They can see my future. I might hit a deer. I better slow down."

I slowed down to 70 kilometers per hour and started praying, about 2 – 3 minutes later, my headlights flashed on two people on the left side of the road, frantically waving their arms. Then, the lights revealed that directly in front of me, approximately 20-feet away, a grey station wagon was stopped in the middle of the road, crossways, blocking both lanes. There were no hazard lights blinking and no room on the road to drive around the car, only a deep ditch on either side of the road. I had less than 10 seconds to react. The second that I saw the scene, I started to freak out inside and thought, "Oh, God! What am I going to do? I am going to hit the car!"

Suddenly, I felt the warmth surround me again. I heard the voice say, "Turn left."

I looked and saw a driveway on my left, but going 70 kilometers per hour, I knew I wasn't going to make it into the driveway. I slammed on the brakes and turned the steering wheel hard to the left. The momentum carried me down the road, parallel to the car blocking the way, and buried the side of my van into the side of the station wagon.

The passenger side of the van was totally smashed, and all the windows shattered. My heart and mind were racing. I was shaking and crying hysterically. I didn't understand why the car was parked blocking the middle of the road.

The couple from the other vehicle came to check on me. I learned that they had been driving in the opposite direction when they hit a deer and their car spun around, and when it stopped; it was blocking both lanes, horizontally. Smoke began coming from their car, and in their shock and fear, they quickly got out of the car, without turning on the hazard lights.

As I calmed down and reflected on what had taken place, I realized I was extremely lucky to be alive. It seemed that everything that had unfolded had been somehow divinely cushioned. I had received a message about the benefit of driving a van over a car, had been warned to slow down, and was guided to turn left. Even though the van was demolished, I could see the beauty and the miracles that happened behind the scenes, which far outweighed the negative appearance of the situation.

The paramedics and police arrived a short time later. As the paramedics were examining me and asking me questions about how I was feeling, I looked up into the sky and marveled in awe at its beauty. It seemed so magical with all the bright stars shining on a clear night, in the dark countryside. I was in a state of bliss, and this concerned the paramedics.

"What are you doing? Is your neck alright?" the paramedics asked, as they examined me for tell-tale signs of brain injury.

"Yes, I am just thanking the Universe for saving my life," I answered.

"Um, are you sure you don't need to go to the hospital?" the paramedic asked in a worried voice.

I reassured everyone that I was fine, and told them that the angels had warned me about this accident. They didn't know what to say, so they just smiled at me. The police officer said, "You are lucky. If you had been going any faster you would not have had time to turn left. If you had hit the car head on, you would have been seriously injured and possibly died on impact, because there are no airbags in your van. Your family is lucky to have you."

I had whiplash and neck and back pain but my heart was full of love. I was extremely grateful to the angels and Source who warned me to slow down.

Although this was a traumatic experience for me, the message was crystal clear. I listened to the divine guidance I heard, and took this as a sign to be true to myself, to honor my calling, and to let go of being a people-pleaser. I made a commitment to myself that from that day on; I would follow my passion and purpose and listen to my intuition.

My injury allowed me to quit my job. It took a full year to recover from the accident with weekly physiotherapy, massage therapy, reiki and chiropractor appointments. I had the freedom to follow my heart and study everything I felt called to learn. No longer feeling pressured to please my family and work in a job I wasn't happy doing, I studied everything with full force and became a certified Reiki Master, Reflexologist, and Hypnotherapist.

With these skills and tools, I began assisting others, just as I had wanted to. I never again worked for someone else; instead I follow my passion and honor my truth.

A Divine Message From A Stranger

"Important encounters are planned by the souls long before the bodies see each other." — *Paulo Coelho*

Later that year, I attended a holistic wellness event. There, I met a very gentle and wise man who taught energy work. He spent a great deal of time talking to me about energy and healing. Then he said, "I can see who you are. Did you know you that had a past-life of Middle Eastern descent? You used to walk with Jesus."

I did not believe in reincarnation, at that time so I thought to myself: "Maybe he is just picking up my energy, because I do pray a lot, and he is associating my energy to a past-life."

Although the thought was logical, it didn't feel right. He had spoken so much truth, I wondered if perhaps reincarnation was truth, as well. Everything else he had shared with me resonated so deeply with me, that I wanted to have a closer look at the idea of reincarnation.

Our conversation was so profound; that I knew it was one of those important moments I would want to revisit later, so I wrote about it in my journal. As I wrote and remembered his words and my feelings, I opened to the possibility of past lives. I knew this meeting had been a divine encounter. What he had said, felt like truth. I wanted to believe him, but I also didn't want to foolishly believe a beautiful fairy tale. I wanted to see if there really was such a thing as a "past-life." I decided that one day I would have a Past-life Regression session and experience for myself what, if any, past-life I had lived before. I didn't want to simply believe what he said without having my own experience in a real session.

Did I actually walk with Jesus in a past-life? If so, had I been a disciple? A family member? A Friend? I don't even know if what the man shared was true. I think it is possible, as I have always felt a connection to Jesus in this lifetime; however, it doesn't really matter, because his message led me to consider new possibilities that I would not have considered otherwise.

I believe that Source used this man to deliver to me a message of love – that I was more than I knew myself to be, and that I was not just a young woman with a finite lifetime. His message opened me up to new possibilities, and I was able to see my eternalness.

Past-Life Regression – My First Experience

After I obtained my hypnotherapist certification, I had the opportunity to learn how to facilitate past-life regression sessions. I still wasn't sure if I believed there was such a thing as past lives, so before I walked through this opening door, I asked God, "Is there such a thing as past lives? Do people really recycle their souls and keep coming back? Why? I am confused. Should I bother taking this class?"

Once I asked, I found myself wondering, "Maybe there is such a thing. Maybe I should take it. What do I have to lose? If past lives are not real, it will be no big deal. At least I am staying open. If they are real, then maybe I can help others with what I learn."

I didn't have any desire to take the class before I asked, only curiosity and openness. Once I asked, I could not stop thinking about the class, and I began to feel a deep desire to take the class. It was as if Spirit was nudging me, and I knew God must want me to take it, so I registered.

In class, I stayed open. I was very curious to learn about my past lives. Even though I didn't know if past lives were true, I wanted to try and experience it. Throughout the day, we practiced with each other, and I got to experience 4 past lives. The processes were very healing for each of us.

Hearing about my past-life and actually seeing it for myself through a past-life regression session were completely different. During the sessions, I relived every important event, felt my feelings, and remembered it like it was yesterday. The experience was unforgettable!

By the end of the class I was vibrating at a new level. I believed in past lives, 100%. I knew the feelings I had felt and the images I had seen were real! It was like watching a television show, and being the main character in the show. From this vantage point, I was able to see the value in every experience I had had, positive and negative, and I learned important lessons from each lifetime. Seeing the larger picture of the lifetime, I was able to forgive those who had hurt me in the past, and see where I was repeating a past pattern in this lifetime, and understand why.

In my first past-life session, I was in Europe, thousands of years ago. I was very tall, slender, and pale with long black hair. I had a twin sister, and I practiced Earth-based spirituality. I saw my sister, and we were in nature, celebrating a full-moon ceremony with other women around a huge bon fire, chanting to the beat of drums. Suddenly, a group of officers appeared out of nowhere and arrested us all. It was our own parents who had turned us in to the authorities, because they thought we were dancing with the devil, and they were afraid of us. The officers stripped us of all our clothes and brutally threw each of us into a hole in the ground. The holes were a sort of cage, measuring approximately 8 feet deep and 3 feet wide. There was a gate made of branches at the top of the hole above us. There was no room to move or sit comfortably, and it was too high to climb out to escape. We were separated and stuck in the ground, naked, alone, in the earth, in the cold, and in the dark. The only thing I could do was look up at the stars and wait for whatever was going to happen.

I remember feeling hungry, afraid, and very cold. It seemed like I was in trapped in the deep hole for approximately 2 weeks with no food and no water, just starving and dying. I felt weak and limp. Eventually, the chief of the police raised me out of the hole and threw me onto a pile of hay, along with my sister and several other women.

I remember the scene vividly. We were lying on top of each other like an abandoned litter of kittens. Too weak to resist or try to escape, all we could do was lie there. The authorities fed the hay with their torches, and as the hay burned, we were engulfed in smoke. Then, still alive, we started to burn.

I was in tears as I watched the scene. The teacher guided me out of that body so I could send love, forgiveness, and healing to that part of myself. Once I withdrew from that body and was watching from above, it was like watching a TV show. I was no longer attached to the situation and could see the larger picture of what had been going on that I was not aware of at the time. I was able to send lots of love to that part of my past.

This experience was very healing, because immediately after this session, I knew that this past-life experience was the root of my fear of my gifts and of the unknown in this lifetime. I also understood that this was where my fear of the dark had come from. This was a huge "Aha!" moment for me.

While in session, I asked God what the lesson was for me in this experience. I heard, "To learn to forgive and be fearless." That made complete sense to me, as in this lifetime, I had been betrayed by my parents and punished for my beliefs and gifts. If I was to learn to forgive and to be fearless, I would need to experience the opposite in order to gain the lesson.

Because I had already experienced the negative repercussions of my beliefs and gifts in a past life, I accepted that it was safe for me to be myself in this lifetime. I accepted that I could let go of my fear of the unknown and embrace my gifts as I discovered them. I knew I could trust that I was safe in this lifetime, and that I could openly and freely share my gifts with others.

After my training, I was excited to offer past-life regression to others. All my friends and family who were open to it had a past-life regression session with me. Each had a powerful experience, as well, and walked away with a better understanding of themselves.

Walking With Jesus

Nine years after the experience in my training class, I attended an event in Toronto where Dr. Brian Weiss, the pioneer of past-life regression, was one of the presenters. He facilitated a group past-life regression session. He said, "Good things happen in a deeper state."

As soon as he said that, somewhere in my consciousness I heard, "Now, you are ready, my child, to hear about your experience of walking with Jesus."

I was surprised, because I had almost forgotten about that divine encounter. Dr. Weiss led us through regression, and what I saw was beyond anything I could have ever imagined.

I saw myself as this elderly, grandmother figure. I had brown skin, long white hair, and dark, chocolate-brown eyes. I felt that I was in my eighties. I wore a long, white gown and brown leather sandals. I felt tremendous love and peace and saw pure white light all over this lifetime. It looked as if a huge divine flashlight was glowing all around me.

I saw Jesus - he was magnificent! He had such a presence, that it is hard to describe. His presence was a very bright, golden light, like seeing an angel. As I looked into his eyes, I felt as if I was gazing at bright stars. He felt very loving, very humble, and so real! I wish I could describe him as dark-haired with brown eyes and tanned skin, but that would be a lie. I didn't see him in the human flesh. I experienced him as a bright light and a powerful love. It was truly divine!

I used to travel alongside him and his disciples to the different villages. I was the babysitter for the children in each town. While Jesus did his healing work on the parents, the elderly, the sick children, and other adults, I would nurture and play with the children. I saw myself in a field of greenery with a large group of children being attracted to me, like a magnet, while their parents and family members crowded around Jesus and his disciples. I watched over the children, keeping them entertained with stories of God, stories of miracles and love. I felt this sense of motherly nurturing and loving energy towards all the children in every town we travelled to. I heard laughter and felt loved. I knew that I had no children of my own in this lifetime, and was a grandmother figure walking with Jesus, serving in a way that only I could serve. I spent my days caring for and playing with the children, and my nights, listening to his teachings.

I saw a spirit guide wearing a dark blue robe. I heard the guide tell me, "You are learning to love all people. You are learning unconditional love for all. This life is all about love."

When I died, I was cradled in the arms of Jesus. It felt as if I was melting away on a soft cloud of peace. I felt his arms around me, as warmth enveloped me. I saw the Holy Spirit all around me, as brilliant white light. I felt unconditional love and the light seemed to smile and kiss my soul. I had no fear of death. I had lived a long time with Jesus, and I was ready.

When Dr. Weiss completed this regression, I was in a state of deep trance and deep, unconditional love. I wanted to run to the stage and tell him what I had just experienced. I wanted to tell everyone, but I knew it wasn't the right time. I heard clearly that I was to just hold this experience in my heart for now.

I realized this might be why I have four children in this lifetime and I really love, and have always loved, other children. I wondered why I had never heard about an old woman travelling with Jesus and watching the children in the Bible. I thought it was probably because in those times, writing about women watching children wasn't a big deal, or maybe those who compiled the Bible didn't think it was important enough to include.

I didn't share this experience with anyone, because I didn't want anyone to diminish it or taint it with their disbelief. I didn't want others to try to persuade me that it was just wishful thinking or create doubt in my mind in any way. I knew this was real. I felt so content with this experience that I embraced the unconditional love I learned from that lifetime.

We Are Divine!

Remember to always follow your divine guidance, even if it doesn't make logical sense. Staying in alignment with your truth will allow your guidance to flow easily. By following your guidance, you will be in the right place at the right time for divine encounters. Sometime you will be on the receiving end, sometimes you will be on the delivering end, and sometimes it will be an exchange. You are Divine, and your connection will allow the Divine to flow through you and bless others in ways we cannot even imagine. I start each day by asking myself, "Where am I going to shine my light today?"

When we follow our spirit, we will always be in alignment with our truth. Each time I prepared myself to write this book, I prayed, grounded myself, and invited my angels, my spirit guides, and Source to shine through me as I wrote. With everyone in my house asleep, just past midnight, I would open and be in the flow. It was like the words and stories just flowed through my fingers to the keyboard.

I just love when I am open to receive the gifts of the Universe and things flow. Things like this happen all the time. We are all One with Source. We are connected to all knowledge and all wisdom. We must trust ourselves, trust our intuition, trust God, and trust all the magical divine encounters!

We are blessed beyond measure, and each of us has our own purpose in life. We must honor our purpose and honor what truly makes us happy in life.

At any time, we can choose to live our lives in Spirit. Whenever we are faced with a problem, we decide if we will respond from Spirit, or from our human self – The Ego. Coming from Spirit is what I aim to do in all my daily activities.

When faced with a situation we want clarity about, we can just ask, "What would my Spirit want?" In the stillness inside, we will be guided or nudged in the direction that is for our highest good.

The more we choose to follow our spirit, the more we will shine pure light around us. When we follow our passion, trust Source, and believe that everything will work out for our highest good, we are embracing our Spirit. We must trust the process of life. It's about the journey – the little magical divine synchronicities, the energy, and the connections.

As I type this book, I am choosing to let go of my ego and follow my spirit. For years I wanted to write a book, but I wasn't ready. I needed to grow more, to trust more, and to believe in myself! So God led me and nudged me, introduced me to people, inspired me, and gave me clear vision as to my purpose in life.

We all have spirit and ego; it's a part of being human. To say, "I do not have an ego," is really saying, "My ego thinks I do not have an ego." Having an ego is part of the human experience. There is nothing wrong or bad about it. We also have free will.

We have the ability to choose what we want to focus on. If we focus on spirit and follow our spirit, we will have more balance in life. We will have more peace in life, more joy, more happiness, and truly be full of love. If we decide to follow our ego, we will have more frustrations, fears, judgment of others and ourselves, anger, mistrust, and unbalanced emotions.

My childhood was full of fear, and my ego was well developed. I needed to experience those fears in order to learn who I really was. I needed to have an ego-based starting point in order to grow, to flourish, to have empathy, and to become who I am today. Through my experiences, I learned to embrace Spirit and choose a better way to live and heal myself. We always have a choice, and each day presents us with moments that are opportunities to make any choice we like.

Each morning, when I say my daily affirmations I say, "I am one with Spirit. I fully embrace my Spirit today." When I repeat this affirmation, I subconsciously program my mind to be more Spirit-centered.

We each have a soul; the soul is who we really are. We are not our bodies, we are not our minds, and we are not our jobs. We are that which is watching our bodies, our minds, and our surroundings. We are the awareness that observes all of life. We are Spirit, and we decide daily how much light we want to shine into the world.

I like to think that Love is Spirit in motion, and Fear is Ego in motion. Sometimes, if we find ourselves in fear, we can ask ourselves, "Where is this coming from – the past or the current life? Is it really my fear or is it an old program I was taught?" While we may or may not get an answer to these questions, the pause shifts our awareness and can interrupt the emotion. From this point, we can make a new choice and choose to open into love instead of acting from fear. As we become aware of our emotions and consciously make efforts to improve, we will find it easier to choose Spirit over Ego on a daily basis. With practice, it has become easier for me to be in Spirit and authentic than to be in ego.

I have been called everything from naïve or a dreamer to rare and unique, but I truly believe we are all the same. I am no different than you. It's our nature to be honest and to walk in truth. As children, we know this truth. We know that being in integrity is our natural state as Spirit. As we grow, we are conditioned by family and society to ignore our truth, our intuition, and our integrity.

Integrity, Truth, and Trust – It's All a Choice

We have seen lies in many places and situations. People we look up to, such as teachers, parents, friends, mentors, and so on may have lied to us before. This subtly programs us to believe that it's perfectly alright to lie – that integrity is not important.

Children know the truth. They are born without fear, and they are born with trust in their hearts. Slowly, they are told how to behave, what to wear, what to say, and what not to say. They stop listening to their own intuition and start wearing a mask, looking outside of themselves for their guidance. That is the way it was for most of us, and it created much pain in our lives.

I made a conscious choice to teach my children to follow their intuition – if someone or something doesn't feel right, listen to that. Don't do something just to fit in, follow your truth, honor yourself, and stand up for your Presence.

Trust is a key ingredient in choosing to walk in Spirit. Trust that everything will be exactly how it is supposed to be. Trust that we are not alone. Trust that God is watching over us. Trust that our hardships will pass, and we will grow from our experiences. We must trust in order to be free from fear. We must trust in order to believe in ourselves. We must trust to follow our truth, our intuition, and our awareness. If we really pay attention to our intuitions, we will be closer to our Spirit- Selves.

I trusted the vision I made when I was fifteen, and that trust gave me a beautiful husband. I didn't know it was a prediction until I met him, but I trusted what my young self said. I trusted that it was a divine intervention. I trusted God during my dark childhood. When I was afraid of the dark, afraid of being bullied and afraid of the abuse in my home, I had trust in my heart. I constantly prayed, and I knew that I wasn't alone.

As I look at my journey, I know that I am blessed to have the level of awareness I have. I am grateful that I am still learning, and I am open to new things. I know that I am a student for life, and I will not be the same person tomorrow that I am right now. I trust that I will evolve. I will grow, and I will inspire others to do the same – to grow, to transform, and to stay in spirit. It really is all about the choices we make. I choose to walk with pure divine love, to radiate divine light, and to stay in spirit today.

Choosing To Be Radiant

Our job is to radiate love, like it's the sun's job to radiate light. We are to shine so brightly that when others see us, they can sense we are amplifiers of love. Start shining your true self, your passion, and your love, and you can create a shift in others' energy fields just by your Presence. Choose to shine your positive light into the lives of everyone you meet. The more we radiate love and light, the more we heal our world, and the more we show others that they can choose to walk in Spirit, too. With a powerful light that fuels humankind, we each have the power to shine. It is our birthright!

Ego Lies and Spiritual Truths – Stepping Into My Power

I became a Reiki master in 2004, but I didn't teach my first class until 2007. I was very insecure about teaching Reiki to others. My ego held me back. My ego would tell me, "You are too young. How can you teach older people when you are still young? People won't take you seriously. You need to be older to start teaching. How can you really have wisdom if you are not old?" I believed my ego.

An older man approached me and asked if I would attune him to Reiki. At first, I declined, thinking that because I was only in my twenties, I couldn't possibly teach someone who is in their 50's. He really wanted me to attune him, so I opened to the possibility that this was Source telling me I was ready to teach, despite my age. As I sat with the idea, it felt right, so I agreed. My ego didn't like that, and I was nervous to teach my first class.

Before the date of the class, I attended a spiritual event and asked the teacher, "How I can let go of my negative thinking that I am too young to be a healer or a teacher?"

What he shared with me was life-changing. He said, "You can be spiritually wise, and physically young. Or you can be physically old, and spiritually like an infant."

That was profound for me. It was exactly what I needed to hear to start believing in my ability to teach and be taken seriously as a teacher.

This calmed my ego, and I chose to trust that Spirit had orchestrated everything perfectly. I embraced my wisdom and taught the class without fear.

By moving from my fearful ego into Spirit, I was able to release my judgments about age and wisdom and the beliefs I had held about them. In Spirit, I was able to see beyond our physical bodies and see the situation as one receiving teachings from another.

Today, my age doesn't hold me back anymore. I teach classes often – in person and by Skype. I am confident and know that I am spiritually wise!

If you ever doubt yourself, remember: You are a beautiful Spirit. God would not give you anything you can't handle. If it is there, you know what to do: trust, choose Spirit, and don't buy into the Ego's fearful lies.

PART V

EMBRACING

"Whatever the present moment contains, embrace it as if you had chosen It." — *Eckhart Tolle*

When we think of the word embrace, what comes to mind? A long hug? Acceptance? Willingness to try new things?

Embracing can mean all these things, and more. To fully embrace life, we must practice being more accepting and loving towards ourselves.

From a young age, we learn that we should put others ahead of ourselves and to deny our own needs. We are not taught to practice self-love. In order to embrace love, however, we must first embrace ourselves. We must practice loving ourselves fully before we can give genuine love to others. We cannot give what we do not have.

Embracing Love of Self

In our younger years, we were told that if we felt good about ourselves, we were self-centered or egotistical, and the disapproving looks of others taught us that this was, indeed, a "bad" thing. Because of this, we need to give ourselves permission to love ourselves, to accept love, and to feel lovable.

When we start loving ourselves, the need for external approval begins to lessen. We stop looking to others to affirm our worth. We begin to know, feel, and be happy with who we truly are.

Self-love focuses on being kind to yourself, refueling your well-being, creating balance, and taking time to feel and accept love. Small acts of self-love help create balance in our lives. It is important to perform these acts, as they nurture and heal us. Taking time to nurture and heal ourselves is practicing self-love. Being patient with ourselves and accepting ourselves as we are right now is an act of self-love. Taking a long bath after a busy day or reading a book that makes the soul smile are ways to practice self-love. Listening to our intuition, following those nudges we get from our inner voice, and trusting ourselves is practicing self-love.

Honoring ourselves and taking the time to do things that make us truly happy is very healing and important to our growth. When we listen to our hearts, our truth, and are kind and gentle to ourselves, we are practicing self-love. When we feel like resting, we need to take time out and rest. When we feel like exercising, we need to take time to move our bodies in a fun way. When we feel like hanging out with friends and eating chocolate, we need to enjoy it – without guilt, without shame, and without judgment – because we are worth it!

When we follow our own dreams and our passions and stop doing things out of pity, obligation, and guilt, we are demonstrating love to ourselves. When we love ourselves, we become the main character of our "movie." We are able to better prioritize our lives, putting our needs ahead of others' "wants," and give of ourselves from a place of joy.

There is a difference between self-love and vanity or narcissism. Vanity and narcissism are not self-love. They are ego-driven characteristics that expose one's lack of self-love.

There are many ways to practice self-love. It can be in the form of getting a massage to relax the body, taking time to journal thoughts and feelings, meditating, or practicing daily positive affirmations.

Most people are their own worst enemy. They are more critical of themselves than they would ever be of others. They constantly berate themselves for minor mistakes, unwanted habits, physical "flaws," and myriad other things. If the self-talk in their heads could be heard by others, we would be astounded by what we heard others say to themselves.

I suffered from a negative body image for years. I judged myself for having big thighs and constantly compared myself to others. I tried countless diets, as I told myself how hard it was to lose weight. It wasn't until after I had my second child that I started to really appreciate my body.

After my second daughter was born, I realized how amazing my body was – how it went from a 9-pound, 20-inch body that had to rely completely on others for everything, to being a full-size body that had just produced a miniature version of itself! The two wee creatures that I loved more than I could have imagined had come from my body! How wonderfully miraculous my body was!

With this new appreciation of my body, I began to love and care for it in a way that I never had before. I started exercising and began feeling confident about myself. I threw away the scales, because I realized that scales could not measure my worth.

I began reframing my thoughts and beliefs about my body. Reframing means "taking a negative statement and rewording it into a positive one." By reframing our thought patterns into positive suggestions, we release negativity and help ourselves feel more loved. This makes it easier for us to give and receive love from others.

For example, if a habitual negative thought is, "I can't stand my thighs. I wish they were skinnier," this thought can be reframed and replaced with, "I am so grateful for my ability to walk. I love my beautiful curves, and I accept myself as I am." We are not our bodies. We are more than just our outside appearances. Remembering this will help us to love and accept ourselves.

When I was a child being bullied, people laughed at me because of my body. I developed negative beliefs about my body. When I became an adult, I needed to let go of these negative beliefs completely and embrace my uniqueness. I had to learn to accept that every curve, dimple and wrinkle of mine is beautiful. Using positive affirmation and hypnosis, I changed the negative programs in my mind to empowering programs so I could love and accept myself fully. Now, instead of thinking, "People will laugh at me," I think, "People are admiring my uniqueness or I love myself unconditionally." Reframing truly helps us embrace ourselves.

Think about the negative beliefs you hold, and write them down. Consider every aspect of yourself – your body, your habits, your character, your past, and your choices. After you have written them down, think about how you can reframe them.

People sometimes feel they shouldn't take time out for themselves, because they believe it would be selfish and they will be judged. We can't just nurture and support others and ignore ourselves. It is important to love yourself first, and then the rest of your life will begin to balance out. Be true to you. Step into love, and embrace your dream, your worthiness, and your goddess self!

Lovely Love Notes

What do you love about yourself? Start making a list of things you love and appreciate about yourself at least once a week. It can include anything you like. I call it "Lovely Love Notes."

Making this list is a good practice for developing the habit of focusing on the good things in life and the positive things about ourselves. Making a weekly list will help us move from judgment about ourselves to appreciation of our uniqueness. Give it a try!

Some examples of MY Lovely Love Notes include:

- I take time for myself and listen to my heart.
- I love my ability to see the beauty in everything life brings.
- I always see the lessons and blessings in life.
- I love my curly hair and my curvaceous, womanly body.
- I love being a mother and learning from my children.
- I love having the wisdom I have, and I practice what I teach.
- I am authentic.
- I am a divine sparkle of light.
- I love my family and feel very blessed.
- I know that everything always unfolds for my highest good.

When you start this fun exercise, you may find it difficult to think of very many things to write. That is okay. You have many years of negative programming to reframe. As you make the lists, however, you will start feeling better about yourself in every way. As you continue with this practice, you will notice the list will grow and change, just as you are growing and changing.

Start today. Take time to write down a few things you love about yourself. This practice of self-love allows you to embrace your body, mind, and spirit.

Embracing Peace

"Peace. It does not mean to be in a place where there is no noise, trouble or hard work. It means to be in the midst of those things and still be calm in your heart." — *Unknown*

When we are at peace, we trust the flow of life, or Source. When we trust Source, we remain in peace. Trusting God will keep us in perfect peace. Even when we experience things that feel like a whirlwind of craziness, if we remember that God has our backs, our peace will return.

Like the analogy of being in the eye of a hurricane, if we stay calm and respond instead of react, staying in the eye of the "storm" around us, we will experience peace and calm and be in the present moment. If, instead, we jump into the storm, into the chaos, where the debris is swirling around, we will lose our peace and become part of the storm. We will add to the drama and the hectic energies of negativity, despair, anger, and frustration.

At times it seems we have no choice and find ourselves getting sucked into a situation; however, we always have a choice. We can choose to jump into the drama, or we can choose to embrace peace – to embrace inner peace, let go, and trust God to surround us with love, light, and clarity.

There are many things we can do to embrace peace within. Meditation is a powerful tool for finding and embracing peace. Meditation will help us still our minds and help create balance in our bodies, minds, and spirits.

Dr. Wayne Dyer said, "Meditation gives you an opportunity to come to know your invisible self. It allows you to empty yourself of the endless hyperactivity of your mind, and attain calmness. It teaches you to be peaceful, to remove stress, to receive answers where confusion previously reigned."

I have found this to be true. I know if I do not meditate regularly, I will not feel like my optimal self.

Starting each day with a simple meditation will set the tone for your day. Finding peace before you embark on your day will help you stay centered and keep you from getting drawn into the drama and chaos you may encounter along the way.

Taking 10 – 15 minutes each morning to find peace can be the key difference between having a good or bad day. Often people claim they don't have time to meditate. I find that funny, because I don't have time NOT to meditate! Having a 10 – 15 minute meditation each morning keeps me from engaging in unproductive and peace-destroying conversations (arguments) and other chaos-laden activities, which end up wasting more time than just 10-15 minutes. A particular family shopping trip provides the perfect example of this.

One evening, I took my 4 children with me shopping. It was near closing time, so other shoppers were hurrying through the aisles. My then two-year old, had missed his nap that day, so he was tired and cranky. The other 3 children were bored and began entertaining themselves by playing around my shopping cart, slowly getting louder and more rowdy. As we waited in the long check-out line, it felt as though everyone was looking at us. A few disapproving looks shot our way. I just smiled and sent silent blessings.

As we left the store, my 2-year old shot out like a bullet, right to the edge of the curb, stopping just short of the parking lot. My eldest ran to him to take his hand and walk him to our van. He began to have a meltdown.

Because I was centered and at peace, I was able to respond instead of react. I said "Awe, looks like you need a big hug," and just gave him a big hug and surrounded him with love.

The bustling shoppers didn't miss the scene, as they hurried to their cars. They watched as my son stomped and cried, and they watched my gentle response. A man smiled at me, as if he was thinking, "I need to remember to do that the next time my son does that!"

Starting my day with meditation and consciously choosing to stay at peace throughout the day helped me during our shopping trip. I was embracing peace. I didn't react to the stress surrounding me, to my son's tantrum, or to other people's judgment. I kept channeling my Divine Essence of Peace. My son fell asleep on the ride home, and I felt like I had demonstrated the mastery of practicing Peace.

It was very calming for me to be in the long lineup and focusing on my children in a loving way, instead of reacting. I know that everything I experience is an opportunity to shine light and grow. I could have gotten concerned about what other shoppers were thinking. I could have gotten drawn into a power struggle with my children. I could have gotten frustrated and upset by my tired son's crankiness and lack of cooperation. Thankfully, because my morning meditation had set the tone for my day, I was able to stay centered and present and flow through the chaos instead of adding to it.

Embracing Clarity

Clarity means to have an understanding or knowing uncluttered by doubts or confusion. When we have clarity, we can better notice our intentions and consciously choose good, positive intentions towards ourselves and others. When we have clarity, we can find it easier to trust Source and know that everything we encounter is showing up to support us and moving us toward what we want.

When we get clear about what we want in life, we can have the life we want. Most of us are more aware of what we don't want than of what we do want – they are two different things. We want more money or time, but we focus on the lack of it. Focusing on what we don't want will always move us in the direction of what we don't want instead of in the direction of what we do want. When we become aware of what we don't want, it is important to get clear about what we do want, and then focus only on that.

It is important that we be clear, because, as the saying goes: "Ask and it shall be given." When we are not clear on what we want, we end up "asking" for a mixture of things – things we want and don't want, at the same time. And whatever we focus on the most, usually what we don't want then shows up in our lives.

You are a creator. You are connected to a divine energy that can manifest anything you choose to focus on. Everything you have in your life at this moment, you have created: your house, your career, your relationships, your hobbies, and your level of freedom. You have chosen these circumstances and experiences through your clarity and focus or lack thereof. You have created your reality. If you're happy with your creation, keep doing what you're doing. If you're not happy with it, you can change it through clarity and focus.

What is it that you want to create in your reality? The clearer you are about what you want to create, the easier it is for you to bring it into your experience.

Making a list may be a good way to see what you are doing in your mind regarding what is wanted and unwanted and where you are putting your focus. When writing down what you do want, you may find your focus shifting to what you don't want. If so, think about its opposite, and write that down, tweaking and fine-tuning it as necessary until it is a match to what you DO want.

Our thoughts create our realities, so in order to attract positive things, we need to be clear and have good intentions. Once we are clear in our thoughts, we begin to clear our emotions, which are the attraction factors of our manifestation abilities. With positive, strong, clear emotions, we can consciously manifest anything we need in our lives.

As a hypnotherapist, I assist others with making changes in their lives through their clarity and focus. I see a high rate of success in my clients who, in addition to our hypnosis session, begin to pay attention to their thoughts and apply positive affirmations to change the way they view things.

By paying attention to our thoughts, we can make sure that if anything comes in that is not in alignment with what we want, such as self-doubt, negative self-talk, gossip about others, or judgments, we can immediately redirect our thoughts into a clear, positive intention that will serve us for the better. Getting rid of any negativity in our lives helps us become clearer in our focus and assists us in living optimally.

There are numerous ways we can embrace clarity, and I encourage you to begin a daily practice, incorporating any or all of the following simple clarity exercises:

- Smudge your energy field using sage or other herbs
- Spend a few minutes focusing on your breathing
- Clear your mind with a few minutes of meditation
- Say positive affirmations, looking into your eyes in a mirror
- Participate in a healing modality that feels right for you

Clarity can also help us see things in a new way. Our willingness for clarity can open us up to other possibilities that we had not considered before. There is always a reason for things happening the way they do, and when we have clarity, we can better know the reason.

Often, things in life don't seem to make sense, or unwanted events blindside us. We tend to come to conclusions about these things or assign meanings to them. Sometimes we may blame karma or luck or think God is punishing us. When we come to a conclusion, we lock into that "reality" about the situation.

When we ask for clarity about the situation, we can "unlock" and better see the greater good to which that event has contributed.

Clarity helps us see that we are exactly where we are meant to be at this moment. Knowing this, we can embrace each moment fully and trust that everything we are experiencing is assisting us in our growth.

Remember be authentic, be honest, and be clear, and you will blossom into the beautiful being that you truly are! We are each seeds of life. We are made to create anything we choose.

Embracing Prosperity

All of us want prosperity, to some degree, however many of us feel it is inappropriate to want prosperity beyond just barely scraping by. We have been taught that to be spiritual we must live no more than just a step above poverty. Spiritual icons, such as Jesus the Christ, Mahatma Gandhi, or Mother Theresa are held up as examples for us to follow. We are told that if we are spiritual, healers, or Lightworkers, then we should not charge for our services, because it is not spiritual to do so. This advice usually comes from 1 of 2 types of people: those who do not want to invest their money into themselves by paying for services, or those who are not allowing prosperity to flow into their lives and likely do not charge for their services.

Prosperity is a form of abundance, and abundance is merely energy. How can it possibly be inappropriate to allow energy to flow to and through us? When energy is not flowing, it is because there are blockages of some kind that we, through our beliefs, have put in place and now have the opportunity to overcome. By changing our beliefs, we can remove the blocks that are preventing the flow of energy, including the energy of abundance and prosperity that we desire, and we can become open to receive.

When we are open to receive, the energy of abundance and prosperity can flow into our lives and give us evidence that we are in alignment with Source. We can acknowledge that we are worthy of receiving prosperity in all of its forms, including money, gifts, experiences, and more.

Many people struggle with allowing prosperity to flow to and through them. We have been taught that money is the root of all evil and that wealthy people are immoral, unjust, unlawful, neglect their families, take advantage of others, or many other qualities that we perceive as "bad" and do not want to become.

Often, these "programs" quietly run in the background and sabotage our financial situations. We somehow have been convinced that we cannot be spiritual and wealthy at the same time; we can only have one or the other.

Nature is abundant. Just notice the abundance that one dandelion puffball can bring – a whole yard full of dandelions! It is the same throughout nature. Abundance abounds! Yet we won't allow nature to have its way with our pocketbooks or bank accounts.

Financial abundance is not a bad thing; instead, it is appropriate, natural, and necessary. The natural flow of prosperity is like breathing: in and out, in and out. Prosperity flows in; prosperity flows out.

A stable financial situation allows us to provide for our families. It allows us to further our educations. It allows us to give support to others in tangible ways. It allows us to contribute to a thriving economy. It allows us to travel and bring our messages and gifts to others that may not have access to us otherwise. It allows us to provide paychecks (and therefore food and shelter) to everyone in the "employment chain" who had a hand in our purchases getting to us, from the farmer to the truck driver to the midnight grocery clerk to the cashier to the guy who collects the shopping carts from the parking lot. Our prosperity contributes to everyone else's prosperity. It is important that we learn how to allow our prosperity to flow.

Each of us has a "prosperity blueprint." It is not ours, exactly; rather it was given to us subtly. Growing up, we watched our families living out their prosperity blueprints and their blueprints became ours. Perhaps we were also given phrases to anchor the blueprints, such as "Money doesn't grow on trees," "We can't afford that," "I'm not made of money," or something similar. Most of our blueprints are negative and based on lack.

When we combine our prosperity blueprints with the other negative beliefs we have picked up along the way, such as "I am not worthy," we almost guarantee that we will keep our prosperity at bay. It does not have to be that way. We can change our prosperity "set point."

Growing up, I watched my mother struggle to support my siblings and me. I watched, as she had to spend her money as soon as she got it – on housing and food and our other needs. My prosperity blueprint included: "Money is hard to get." "To have money, one must make a lot of sacrifices." "Money does not last."

Without knowing it, I was being programmed for my own future financial situation. In my young adult life, this was exactly how my finances played out. There was never enough money, and what I had was spoken for before it made it to my hands.

As I learned more about the subconscious "programming" we get in childhood and how to make conscious, positive changes to those beliefs, I began to change my prosperity blueprint. As I made those belief changes, my financial situation began to change, too.

When I started my holistic healing business, I also struggled with the belief that wealth and spirituality cannot mix. I believed that God had given me these gifts; therefore I should give them away to others instead of charging for them, especially to friends and family. I disliked telling people how much my services cost and felt guilty asking for payment. I constantly gave away my services despite knowing that others were charging the same amount, and they were just as spiritual. I felt unworthy of the prosperity that was trying to enter my life and was resisting the flow of abundance that was right on my doorstep.

One day, I met an angel, disguised as a client, who came to me for reiki treatments. I felt an immediate soul connection. In a relatively short time, we became good friends. As we moved from a business relationship into a friendship, I began to feel badly about charging her for reiki treatments. I discussed this with her, and she helped me change my belief so I could start accepting the prosperity that was trying to make its way to me.

She said, "You are undervaluing and underpaying yourself. You need to stop giving discounts because you are worth the fee you charge. Every time you give a discount, you are telling the universe, "I am not worth it. I am not good enough." You put so much time, energy, and love into everything you do. You are an expert in your field. Just because it feels natural and comes easy for you to work with your hands and provide these services, it doesn't mean your work is any less valuable than other professionals. Look at surgeons. They work with their hands, too, and no one expects them to give them a discount. Stop giving discounts! If you want to set a special rate for family and friends, then do that, but accept the abundance that is flowing into your life!"

She suggested that I make a list of everything I had studied, how much time I had put into each thing I had studied, how long each course was, and how much everything had cost me. She said that once I saw it written down, it would show that I am worth the fees I charged for my services because I had earned it. She added, "Every year you are worth more, because you have another year of experience."

I made the list, and once I saw all the years, money, and time I had devoted to becoming the person I am today, I was able to begin embracing my prosperity. Through her, I was able to allow myself to see the value I truly bring to my clients. She taught me that it is appropriate to accept payment and to allow prosperity to flow to me. She helped me see that not only do I deserve it, but that I have earned it and therefore have no reason to feel badly at all.

I realized that when I do not charge for my services, people may not value my services, and they may not take me seriously as a businesswoman. It allows others to take advantage of my kindheartedness and my desire to help others move through their struggles with grace. I realized that when I do not charge for my services, I am actually dishonoring my gifts and myself.

I also came to realize that what appeared to be charging money for my services was actually exchanging energy with my clients. The energy I offered came in the form of whatever service I was providing, and the energy they offered in exchange came in the form of printed paper that I could later use to exchange for groceries or gasoline, additional exchanges of energy.

As I started letting go of my fear and judgment of prosperity, I started having more clients. Now, I embrace prosperity, and I answer the question, "How much will it cost?" with confidence. I have regular fees that I charge for services, alternative energy exchange options for a few clients when I feel guided, and a set rate for family and friends. This feels right for me and demonstrates respect for my business and myself, thereby commanding respect from those wanting to access my services.

Thinking back to when I first started my business and how I struggled to get just 1 client, I can see how far I have come in my own journey to prosperity. My prosperity blueprint made me unable to trust the process of an energy exchange or believe that prosperity was even possible for me. Today, I know that financial freedom is our birthright, and there is a flow of prosperity for anyone who taps into it!

When I changed my blueprint from, "I need to struggle hard to earn money," to "Money flows easily into my life," I noticed an increase in my business. Instead of increasing my advertising, my new prosperity blueprint sends out vibrational frequencies that tell the Universe I am ready and open for abundance to flow into my life easily and effortlessly. My fear-based and lack-focused prosperity blueprint shifted to an abundance-centered and allowing-focused blueprint.

When we ask for what we want, we will receive according to our prosperity blueprints. When we change our disempowering beliefs about prosperity and worthiness, we can change our prosperity blueprints into ones that will allow us to have the abundant and prosperous lives that we desire.

Embracing Difficulties

"The gem cannot be polished without friction, nor can man be perfected without trials." — *Chinese proverb*

In an earlier chapter, I shared some of the difficulties I had growing up and some of the challenges I had to release in order to allow me to feel love and let go of fear. Letting go of the pain of our past experiences and accepting them as blessings in our life is nothing less than a miracle. It is not common or easy to reframe our experience as "victim" to one of "student" or "co- creator," but it is healing, and it is also true.

Every situation in our lives is here to serve us, to mold us, to make us stronger, and help us develop our spiritual awareness. Like the Chinese proverb states, with tribulations, we are polished and become diamonds.

God always has our back, our hearts, and our spirits. We just need to go with the flow and trust that no matter how hard things become, we are never alone! Anytime you are faced with a challenge, remember that you are loved, and that you are never given something you can't handle.

Difficulties can be a way we develop new skills, or they can be a way we show ourselves the level of mastery we have acquired. Troubles are never punishment from God or evidence of sin or wrongdoing; rather they are opportunities to draw closer to the Divine and access resources necessary to manage the challenge with ease.

Too often, we mistake our struggles for things going awry. We lose sight of the gifts that they truly are and focus on how differently things are going than what we had planned. We begin to see ourselves as victims of things out of our control. We may fight and push against what is happening, or we may helplessly give up.

If we can take a more observer point of view, we are less likely to get swallowed by the fear, anger, and chaos. We can assess the situation from a non-attached point of view and ask better questions.

Instead of asking, "Why is this happening to me?" we can ask, "What has this come to teach me?" When we view challenges as our friends, we can move through them faster and with less pain than when we view them as intruders that are victimizing us.

There are 2 sides to every coin, and we can look at one side or the other. So it is with our circumstances. How we view them is our decision. We can choose to be angry or upset and feel like a victim, or we can embrace the difficulties, choose to go with the flow, accept or release what is happening, and be open to see the lesson or opportunity for growth that is presenting.

When we accept what is happening and let go of how we think we need things to be, we make room for more divine love in our lives, and we can learn and grow through whatever is happening with more grace. Our difficulties provide fertile ground through which we can grow and evolve in ways never imagined.

My Son, My Teacher - Living With Allergies

We all have unwanted events and circumstances in our lives. I am a firm believer that everything happens for a reason. I believe that everything I experience is showing up to assist me in my growth and evolution – especially the unwanted things.

A powerful unwanted experience became one of my greatest opportunities to learn and grow, and my young son became my teacher.

After returning home from a shopping trip, I sat my 18-month old son at the table with a snack of pesto and toast to enjoy while I put away the groceries. As he ate, I noticed his lips began to swell. Not knowing what was happening, I kept watching and noticed he began to develop hives.

I gave him some Benadryl and thought he was going to be fine. Then he looked at me wide-eyed and said, "Me choke! Me choke!" I quickly gave him a dose of the inhaler I use when his asthma begins to act up. The inhaler did not provide the relief that it usually did, and I realized what was happening was very serious, so I called 9-1-1.

My precious little one swelled beyond recognition. He resembled "The Thing" from the Marvel movie "Fantastic Four." The ambulance arrived, and the paramedics rushed in.

Their quick assessment revealed that my baby's oxygen level was down to 90%, which meant he was really struggling to breathe. His throat was closing as it swelled. He was in the middle of a full-blown anaphylaxis shock.

The paramedic immediately administered an Epipen shot and hooked my son up to oxygen and several high-tech machines that monitored his heart. He was in such crisis that he needed two Epipen shots to counter the allergic reaction and get his breathing and oxygen level back on track. We were taken to the hospital and had to spend the night to ensure he was stable.

At the hospital, the Doctor said, "If you had gotten here any later, it would have been too late."

Like any mother would be, I was in fear mode through the whole nightmare. Although I was unable to stay grounded and centered, as I watched my son inch closer and closer to death, I used my tools to help me stay connected with Source as much as possible. I kept praying, surrounding us with Reiki, and calling on Archangel Raphael for healing.

A few days later, my son was seen by an allergist who sent us to have blood tests done to see what exactly he was allergic to. When the results were in, we discovered he is highly allergic to all tree nuts, (pine nuts) and fatally allergic to peanuts. Pine nuts are in pesto sauce, which explained his reaction, and his sensitivity to peanuts is so severe that he can go into anaphylaxis shock from just touching a peanut or peanut residue.

It took me a few days to adjust to this news, as I realized how things would need to change in order to ensure my son's safety. I recognized that while I would need to become more focused and aware of things that were in my son's environment, I would need to be mindful and not cross the line into allowing fear to control our lives.

My head was full of "what ifs:" What if he kisses a girl as a teenager, and she has eaten peanuts? What if he is at a friend's house, and I am not there with him to protect him, and he accidentally has peanuts?" I knew that it was going to be a challenge to stay in Spirit and trust whatever the future held and go with the flow instead of living in fear.

I began searching for reasons why this happened and began blaming myself for his allergies. For a while, I tortured myself with thoughts like, "It must be because I ate a lot of peanuts when I was pregnant with him."

Eventually, I was able to find peace. My metaphysical spiritual beliefs assisted me in letting go of fear and blame and began accepting my son's allergies as they were. I believe that no matter what happens in the future, God won't give me anything I can't handle. I also believe that before we come to Earth, we, as souls, choose our experiences – our parents, our families, and our paths. I began to trust that my son had chosen to have this experience. Perhaps he had decided, "Hmmm I am going to go to Earth School. If I want to come back home to the Spirit world, how should I exit the Earth Plan? Well, I will pick peanut allergies. That way if things get too much to handle on Earth, I can have a quick exit point back home."

Reframing things in this way helped me let go of my fear and the need to control my son's future and begin trusting that everything – including my son's allergy and his future – was exactly as it should be. It also helped me accept the possibility that my son may have a fatal reaction one day and that, should that happen, even that would be exactly as it should be.

Today, my son is managing well with his allergies. He takes responsibility, and always asks, "Does it have any nuts?" before accepting anything edible from anyone. He reads labels on foods and gets so excited when something is peanut-free!

My son was my teacher, and took my spiritual awareness to a new level. His allergies put my faith to the test – did I truly believe what I purported to believe? He stretched me outside of my comfort zone regarding how much I was willing to trust God.

My son taught me to let go of blame and to accept that some things have nothing to do with me and that I can't control everything. He taught me to trust that his path is between him and God and that I had to let go of my expectations and fears and to trust that everything is under Divine Guidance.

My son taught me to let go of anger, to stop perceiving as a victim, and to put things in perspective. There were times I thought, "Why me? I am a good person. I don't deserve this," and "Why him? He's just a baby, and he is such a good boy!"

I shared my anger and frustration with my husband, and in his wisdom, he answered me with, "Why not you?" That was my reality check. My husband was right. Why not me? Why did I think I shouldn't have this experience? Why did I perceive this as unfair and as something we should not have to deal with? These questions lead me to a new level of inner exploration, self-awareness, and spiritual growth. I came to realize that things could be a lot worse, and I had a choice about how I was going to view this. Aside from the allergies, he was a smart, strong, and healthy boy. I realized I needed to focus on what was going right and be grateful for his good health, strong body, and sharp mind.

My son taught me acceptance and going with the flow. I had no control over his allergies. I could fight against it, but that would not change things. I could become hyper-vigilant about my son's environment and "bubble-wrap" him to protect him, leaving him unprepared to navigate a peanut-ridden world in the future.

Instead, I asked myself, "What am I learning with this experience?" I was reminded that everything is in God's hands, and the outcome is under Divine Guidance. Death is inevitable for all of us, and embracing each moment is what life is about. My role is to educate myself and educate my son. The unfolding of his life is between him and God.

My son taught me to turn from fear to love during challenging times, because love heals fear. Turning to love helped me to let go of my fear and to trust that everything is going to be all right. God is love, and love is the best medicine. May our lives be filled with love and may each of us trust that we are not given anything we cannot handle. This poem gave me comfort during these times.

> *"There is no difficulty that enough love will not conquer; No disease that enough love will not heal;*
> *No door that enough love will not open; No gulf that enough love will not bridge;*
> *No wall that enough love will not throw down; No sin that enough love will not redeem.*
> *It makes no difference how deeply seated may be the trouble, How hopeless the outlook,*
> *How muddled the tangle, How great the mistake;*
> *a sufficient realization of love will dissolve it all.*
> *If only you could love enough you would be the happiest and most powerful being in the world."*
>
> — Emmet Fox

When we embrace difficulty, it cannot bring us down. Each difficulty carries a lesson, and if we are willing to embrace them, each experience will help us become a better version of ourselves.

Embracing Health

Embracing health encompasses every aspect of our selves: a healthy mind, a healthy body, a healthy spirit, and an overall healthy lifestyle. There are many things we can do to become healthier. For us to be truly healthy, we need to have balance in these areas and intentionally focus time and energy into creating and maintaining our health.

As we work on these areas, we create an overall healthy lifestyle. The specifics of this vary from person to person. Instead of trying to follow a certain regimen, it is important to listen to your inner guidance. It's fun and helpful to join with friends to support each other as you all work on lifestyle change, however, the same approach may not work for all of you. Having a support team is a great idea; just recognize that your inner guidance knows the best way for you to accomplish your goals.

For me, I enjoy working out, which includes a variety of activities, including: belly dance, kettle bells, free weights, and boxing. I work out because it makes me feel happier, healthier, and physically stronger. Working out produces natural endorphins that make me feel happy, and this naturally encourages me to stay consistent with my workouts. My muscles become stronger, my endurance and stamina increase, and my overall health improves. Being present and aware in my body and embracing it as it is, I notice subtle changes, and these changes further motivate me to remain consistent with my workouts.

Noticing these changes in my body encourages me to eat healthier, too. I tend to eat more greens, fruit, and vegetables when I workout and less convenience or "junk" foods. There is something about the time and energy I devote to loving my body and my Self through working out that makes me want to provide a higher grade of fuel for my body, and it becomes a self-perpetuating cycle for me.

We are surrounded by messages of lifestyle change, and it can be overwhelming and even costly to consider: gym memberships, equipment, special foods, protein shakes, meal replacements, etc. It doesn't have to be that way. Lifestyle change can be simple and can happen with "baby steps." Committing to a single change and following through with it on a daily basis is all it takes.

Every day, try doing something that makes you feel healthier. Maybe it's starting to move your body more, or choosing to make a green smoothie, or choosing to not have the extra serving of dinner or dessert. Every day we have to decide what we want to consume. A simple decision of rice and vegetables instead of frozen pizza or parking further from the door of the grocery store than usual in order to walk a little more can be the start of a great shift. Think about what you would like to do to make yourself feel healthier each day. Consider things like "addition" or "substitution" instead of "elimination."

When we eliminate something we enjoy, we begin to feel deprived and will eventually rebel against ourselves and "cheat" or abandon our new plan. If we substitute something else instead, it's easier to honor our commitments to ourselves. We can give ourselves permission to have the item that is tempting us if we want, and then choose something else. For example, we can think, "Yes, I can have a piece of cake if I want it. However, I'm going to have a fruit salad instead." The subtle difference between allowing oneself the freedom to choose vs. being forced to stick to a method of deprivation can help us stay committed to ourselves.

Unfortunately, many of us gauge our health by our weight. Good health is not about the numbers on the scale; it's about how your body feels inside and out! Scales are just a way to know our relationship with gravity, nothing else.

When I was a teenager, I weighed 75 lbs less than I do as an adult. I ate loads of sweets, drank gallons of pop, and had a nice body, but I was very unhealthy. I had chronic back pain, no strength or flexibility, and had no confidence. Almost two decades later, I weigh more than I did in those days, however I do not have any back pain, I have great strength and flexibility, and I radiate self-confidence. Today, I am mindful about what I eat. I do not drink pop. I work out, and I feel healthier and more beautiful and powerful than ever! I accept my body no matter how much I weigh or what size I am. I know that the number on the scale doesn't mean I am a healthy person; what I choose to consume and how I choose to live is what makes me a healthy person.

When we think of changing our lifestyles and being consciously selective about what we chose to consume, we tend to focus on foods. While the quality and types of food we consume is important, it is equally, and possibly even more important, that we also consider what we are consuming mentally and emotionally or vibrationally. The shows we watch, the conversations we participate in, and the people we surround ourselves with also affect our health.

Current research tells us that over 90% of diseases are stress-related. How many of us stress-eat? How many of us let our stress or emotional discontent determine the choices we make – indulge in ice cream, go shopping, yell at someone, drink alcohol, or other action that distracts us from what we are feeling? This demonstrates the importance of monitoring our mental, emotional, and vibrational diets.

Good health requires a holistic approach and takes all aspects into consideration. Once I learned that, my approach to good health changed. Instead of counting calories, portioning my meals, and making sure I spent a certain amount of time with my heart beating at a certain rate, I began to listen to my inner guidance and include all aspects of life.

Today, my mind is alert, my body is strong, and my spirit is soaring! I am truly healthy! Like an eagle, I am flying high on life, and I am embracing my health. I am blessed to have the body I have. It is a magical vehicle for my soul!

PART VI

STRENGTH

"Don't die with your music still inside you. Listen to your intuitive inner voice and find what passion stirs your soul."   - Dr. Wayne Dyer

We each have gifts and talents that we need to embrace and find the strength to allow ourselves to shine. Not physical strength, rather the inner strength that comes from knowing and trusting our guidance and knowing and trusting that everything we experience is conspiring for our greatest good. When we discover and utilize this strength, we can live our lives with passion and on purpose.

Each day, we have the opportunity to change and create our futures. It is our inner strength that allows us to blossom into the fullness of who we truly are and bring our gifts fully to the world, as we intended when we began our Earth journey. We can achieve amazing things when we remember who we really are – a spark of creation, a piece of the Universal Consciousness – and access our inner strength.

Do you have an idea of something you want to create or experience but keep putting it off? We have all experienced this at some point in our lives. We desire to take action and live our dreams, but that is as far as some of us will allow things to go. We stop at that point and won't give ourselves permission to make or allow things to happen. We give up our dream and sacrifice our greatest desires, because we give more power to our fear than to our dreams.

I meet numerous people who have great creative ideas, but they lack the inner strength to take action. I, too, used to struggle with that.

Dr. Wayne Dyer has been very instrumental on my journey. He was the positive male role model that I did not have when I was growing up. His words have guided and encouraged me to express the "music" inside me and to allow it to flow without worrying about what others may think. It has been easier said than done, but as I drew upon my inner strength, I was able to focus on my dream, listen to my inner voice, and trust the flow as things unfolded and presented to me along the way.

Today, I am so accustomed to following my intuition and expressing the passion stirring my soul, that it seems foreign for me to even consider holding myself back from this way of being.

Tony Robbins says, "If you continue to do what you have always done, you will continue to get what you have always gotten." What we choose to do today can change the rest of our lives. We can choose to continue to do what we've always done or we can choose to draw upon our inner strength to go in a new direction and move toward our dreams and goals.

Think about a time that you had to rely on your inner strength to accomplish something. It seemed that everything in you wanted to take the familiar or easy road, but something inside spoke up, and you were able to find the strength to do something different. Maybe it was to stand up to a bully, say "no" to a delicious treat, face a fear, or leave an abusive relationship. It is likely that after you did this, you felt a rush as your personal power returned to you. Perhaps you noticed that when you were faced with the same situation later, it was easier to make the choice you really wanted.

We are all faced with challenges of varying degrees that allow us the opportunity to choose what is best for us and may require that we call upon our inner strength to make the choice and hold to it. As we work on loving ourselves, it becomes easier to access that inner strength.

When we begin accessing our inner strength, we begin to truly love our lives. We begin to live our lives to the fullest and with no regrets.

Imagine being in your 70's, 80's, or even 90's. Would you rather be telling stories about your life – your adventures and time when you did things you thought you could not do? Or do you want to wonder what would have happened if you had acted on an idea, written that book, had more confidence, or taken more risks? Do what is necessary today so you will be able to when the time comes. Your future begins with what you do today. Plant the seeds for your dreams, build your foundation with daily gratitude, and trust that what you plant will grow.

What if every idea that comes to us was really a prayer being answered? We constantly pray for more abundance in all areas of our lives – health, love, family, finances, etc. Our prayers are usually answered in unexpected ways. Sometimes it is an idea that pops into our heads, overhearing something that inspires us to start something new, or someone appearing in our lives at just the right moment. We may doubt that our prayers are heard or are going to be answered, but we can have faith and know that we are not alone. Our prayers are always answered: sometimes the answer is "yes," sometimes it is "no," and sometimes it is "wait." If everything is working together for our highest good, and God answers in mysterious ways, then we can trust that our prayers are being answered, whether we recognize the answer when it appears or not.

If we open our eyes to see everything as an answer to prayer, even if we don't see how it could be, we will begin to notice how everything is working together and moving us toward the vision we have for ourselves. This will lead us to trust God more and assist us in finding our inner strength when we need it. If we are supported in our everyday things, we can know that in the tough times, when we need to draw on our inner strength, comfort zone, it's easy to allow our fear to keep us "safe." This actually inhibits our growth and sabotages the dreams we have for ourselves. Instead of buying into the fear, we can question it. What's the worst that can happen? When we explore the worst-case scenarios, we usually find their validity falls apart. Even if an unwanted event occurs, everything is temporary and "This, too, shall pass."

When we entertain the fear and perceived horror that could unfold from our choice to step out of our comfort zone, we eliminate the possibility of finding our inner strength. We cannot look two places at once.

Do you want to live in fear and "safety" (better said: stagnation) or move into growth and change? Silence your fear and focus on the dream that lies beyond the next step, and then take the action! Once you do it, you will be happy you did.

Many of us are surrounded by naysayers – people who have given up on their dreams and are disturbed that we are pursuing ours. The more we value their opinions, the more we allow them to have a negative influence on us, and the more we allow them to instill doubt and fear in us. We need to be more selective about the company we keep and what we share with whom.

When we spend time with people with positive attitudes and outlooks, who believe in our vision, it is easier to take steps time with negative people and changing the topic instead of engaging when they want to discuss the dreams that we are nurturing, will help us move toward making our dreams a reality.

We all encounter someone that gives us unwanted advice. Instead of allowing it to gain a foothold in our minds and feed our own fears, we can just let it go. We can know that they are actually sharing the fears and concerns they had about the dreams they abandoned. Their position and opinions truly have nothing to do with us or our dreams.

When I get overwhelmed or even frightened by my vision for myself, I comfort and remind myself, "Oprah, The Dalai Lama, Mother Teresa, Tony Robins, Dr. Wayne Dyer, Nelson Mandela, and Maya Angelou are all people just like me. They, too, had a vision and a dream. They did not let anyone stop them, not even their own fears. They believed in themselves and took action to accomplish what they desired. They followed their intuition and had the inner strength to not let others bring them down. Look at them now! Their names are unforgettable. They have each created such a tremendous shift on our planet just by taking action and following their hearts. They have each made a huge impact on our world and will always be remembered."

Remembering these truths helps pull me out of my overwhelm or fear and into a place where I am able to see things from a different perspective. From my new vantage point, I am able to better access the strength to take the steps I have been stopping myself from taking.

Those who inspire us – our heroes and role models – are just like us. We like to think of them as lucky or blessed, but honestly, what makes them different? We all started out fresh and new, with nothing, as babies. We all had our own versions of difficulties and challenges throughout our lives. We all had people who discouraged us along the way. We all breathe the same air. We all make choices everyday that lead us toward or away from our goals and dreams. We can all achieve what we desire if we truly want to – if we are willing to take the steps necessary to allow our dreams to unfold.

No one is more special or deserving than another. Instead, some of us are more willing – more willing to question our negative beliefs, more willing to face our fears, more willing to trade our old, disempowering programming for new empowering programming, more willing to love ourselves, more willing to abandon the familiar and step into the unknown, and more willing to trust the dream that is calling us forward.

As a teen, I had low self-esteem and didn't have anyone I could talk to about things that were troubling me. I silently called out for support. Not long after, I discovered a poem by Maya Angelou. It was so perfect for what I needed at the time. I cut it out of the magazine, glued it into my school agenda, and read it almost daily to help build my inner strength.

Phenomenal Woman

*Pretty women wonder where my secret lies.
I'm not cute or built to suit a fashion model's size.
But when I start to tell them,
They think I'm telling lies.
I say,
It's in the reach of my arms
The span of my hips,
The stride of my step,
The curl of my lips.
I'm a woman
Phenomenally.
Phenomenal woman,
That's me.*

*I walk into a room
Just as cool as you please,
And to a man,
The fellows stand or
Fall down on their knees.
Then they swarm around me,
A hive of honey bees.
I say,
It's the fire in my eyes,
And the flash of my teeth,*

The swing in my waist,
And the joy in my feet.
I'm a woman
Phenomenally.
Phenomenal woman,
That's me.

Men themselves have wondered
What they see in me.
They try so much
But they can't touch
My inner mystery.
When I try to show them
They say they still can't see.
I say,
It's in the arch of my back,
The sun of my smile,
The ride of my breasts,
The grace of my style.
I'm a woman
Phenomenally.
Phenomenal woman,
That's me.

Now you understand
Just why my head's not bowed.
I don't shout or jump about

Or have to talk real loud.
When you see me passing
It ought to make you proud.
I say,
It's in the click of my heels, The bend of my hair,
the palm of my hand, The need of my care,
'Cause I'm a woman Phenomenally. Phenomenal woman, That's me.

– Maya Angelou

I thank Maya Angelou for planting the seed in my mind that I, too, could be a "Phenomenal Woman," because now I am! Remember that you are a Phenomenal Being, as well, whether a woman or a man. Go spread your mystery to others! Shine so brightly that others will want to understand what it is you are sharing! Embrace yourself fully and be a Phenomenal Being! You can create the life you truly want. You, and only you, are the master of your life!

Just Be You

Another way for us to build our inner strength is to practice being authentic with ourselves and listening to that quiet voice of guidance that lies within us. We each have our unique talents, strengths, energy, purpose, and passion. The more we align with our truth, the happier we will be with our lives. The more we allow ourselves to be our authentic selves, the more we invite others to do the same. We do not need to pretend to be someone we are not, or try to fit in with our society. We did not come to Earth to be a copy of someone else; we came to bring our special gifts in our unique packages. When we compromise ourselves in order to gain acceptance or approval from others, we do the whole world a disservice, especially ourselves, as we shortchange ourselves on many levels – our health, our spiritual life, and our overall satisfaction with life.

In my holistic healing practice, I am constantly encouraging others to be true to themselves. Many clients I treat have difficulty speaking their truths, listening to their hearts, and being authentic. Often tears come out during healing sessions because they have been holding on to their true feelings for a long time, and they finally feel safe enough to share their truths.

Being ourselves and speaking our truths feed our souls with positive energy and align us with Source. When we speak our truths, we are being our authentic selves.

Being authentic honors Source. Playing small, rejecting parts of ourselves, or being something different from who we really are in order to fit in, suggests that the Creator didn't know what She/he was doing or somehow made a mistake. We are divine beings worthy of being authentic and honest with ourselves, the people around us, and the universe. We do not need to pretend or defend. If you are faced with someone who makes you feel like you need to defend yourself, prove yourself or pretend to be different then who you truly are; then listen to your body. Walk away. Just be you, period.

When we are authentic, expressing our truths, and being ourselves, we are in alignment with the divine within. We are expressing the uniqueness of who we are. We are all special and have our own truths, passions, teachings, experiences, and love to share with others. Being honest and following our inner guidance is what makes us amazing sparkles of light.

By being authentic and celebrating our own truths, we are thanking God for the gift of our beingness. Each of us exists in this time and space for a reason. We each have a purpose that is intended to synergetically impact our world. We are not supposed to dim ourselves, but rather express ourselves as the divine beings that we are!

In my early twenties, I worked as an extra in TV shows. It was a fun and easy job, and I met many people from all walks of life. A female co-worker one day asked me, "What is your story? People that are pretty like you are not usually friendly. Why are you so friendly?"

I was surprised by her question. Since beginning my healing journey, everyone in my world was friendly. I told her "I am always like this. I am just being me."

We continued visiting. As our conversation moved into talking about health, I shared with her how I lost a hundred pounds after my first child was born. Then she said "Oh! Now, that makes sense. You used to be fat. That's why you are friendly."

I found her perception interesting. In her world, fat women were friendly and pretty women were unfriendly. Because I was pretty and friendly, she could not make sense of the situation, because it did not match her belief system. When I said I had lost weight, she decided I must have been fat before, deleting the fact that I had been pregnant. To her, this explained why I was friendly.

I answered, "That's not true. It doesn't matter what size someone is or how someone looks. What matters is what's in the heart."

This was more than she could accept. She was able to reframe things to accept that I was pretty and friendly, but this response further conflicted with her beliefs, and she was not ready to consider this possibility. And that was the end of the conversation.

This woman judged me because of how I looked. She assumed I would be a certain way simply because of my appearance. This concept was foreign for me, because I don't do that. I also don't worry about what people will think of me. I am just me, no matter what. It doesn't matter what size I am, what color my hair is, or where I am or who I am talking to. I am always myself. What you see is what you get. I have learned that it is easier to be real instead of pretending to be different in order to fit into a situation."

Be who you are, not who you think your family or someone else wants you to be. Be yourself, and listen to your heart, because at the end of the day, if we can't be honest with ourselves, how can we be honest with others?

Inner Strength – Listening to my heart

In an earlier chapter, you read about how I manifested my husband. My family did not accept our relationship in the beginning. They tried everything they could to separate us. I had to access my inner strength in order to trust my intuition about him, no matter what my family said or how hard they pushed to get me to leave him.

We both were almost eighteen years old when we began dating. Both of us were born in Canada, but because he is black and I am Latina, my family didn't approve of our relationship. My family was not pleased that I was dating someone of another race.

"Why are you with him? You deserve better."

"You should break up with him and focus on school."

"You do not know what real love is. He is only your first boyfriend."

"You are too young to know what love is."

"He is not the one for you. Stop listening to a silly coincidence; you did not predict your soul mate!"

I heard things like this from my cousins, my aunts, my uncles, my mom, and even my grandma. I did not let their opinions distract me from my truth. I knew with all my heart that he was the one for me.

It was difficult to stand in my truth while constantly being pummeled with their negativity and doomsday predictions. I loved my family and appreciated their concern for me. I was happy with my boyfriend and wanted them to be happy for me. They could only imagine the worst and shared their views at every chance. I knew they meant well, yet I knew the truth: we were soul mates.

I loved him. I loved his essence, his energy, and his pure heart. I knew he was the one!

To me, it didn't matter how he looked, what color he was, or what anyone said. What mattered to me was the knowing I had in my heart. I held to that truth and did not let anyone sway me. After ten years, my family finally accepted our relationship.

We loved each other then, and we love each other now. I am happy, blessed, and grateful that I had the strength to listen to my heart and not outside sources. I can't imagine my life any other way!

PART VII

SENSUALITY

"Get out of your head and get into your heart. Think less, feel more."
- *Osho*

Sensuality means using all of our senses for pleasure – our senses of touch, sound, smell, taste, and sight. Using our senses is something that assists us in having deeper connections – with nature and other people, but especially with ourselves.

We are sensual beings. We experience life through our senses on a daily basis. We feel joy, pain, laughter, and love through our senses. We can also use our senses to heal ourselves – to balance our bodies, minds, spirits, and emotions.

People often confuse sensuality with sexuality. They are different things but complement each other very well.

Sensuality is focused on the senses and experiencing pleasure through the senses. Most of us find pleasure and enjoyment in the feel of the soft fur of a kitten, fingertips massaging our scalps, the soothing warmth of soaking in a bathtub, the sound of water flowing gently over rocks, the smell of freshly baked bread or cookies, or the taste of a decadent dessert. These are all sensual experiences. While sexuality can be incorporated into sensual activities, sensuality does not require any aspect of sexuality.

Young children, even infants, will discover and begin touching their genitals. For them, this is not a sexual activity; it is a sensual activity. It feels good.

Adults almost always immediately equate this activity with sexuality, due to their own sexual experiences. They confuse sexuality with sensuality and often shame children for enjoying a sensual experience. This can lead to lifelong shame associated with sexuality, sensuality, and genitals. These well-meaning adults inadvertently create problems that the children may carry well into adulthood.

Young children do not have the reasoning skills, understanding, or life experience that adults do and therefore interpret this shaming in ways adults cannot predict. They can begin to form negative beliefs about their bodies, their inherent goodness, their value, and many other negative beliefs about themselves that will play out later in life. Many of us are living with those same beliefs today because of the way adults handled the situation when we began exploring sensuality as children.

Throughout history, there have been numerous products and practices implemented in order to interfere with a child's healthy exploration of sensuality which adults mistake for sexuality. The underlying message has been: sensuality is sexual and sexuality is shameful. The logical association that is made is: my genitals are shameful; feeling good through my genitals is shameful; I am shameful. Shame can lead to sexual dysfunction in adulthood.

It's not shameful to enjoy the sensual or sexual part of being a divine human being or to have our sacred hot spots caressed. Being in a loving, healthy, and compassionate relationship with a partner creates an energy that is strong and passionate.

It is said that sexual energy is the strongest energy on our planet. It's the beginning of our existence, our entry into the earth plan. It's such a powerful creative energy force that, if one is able to focus on something she would like to manifest while having an orgasm, it's like putting an amplifier on the desire. Incorporating orgasmic, creative energy can allow the desire to come to fruition sooner than it would by only performing general manifestation exercises, such as creating a vision board.

In an effort to keep me pure and chaste, my mother sheltered me from information about sex. I wasn't allowed to attend the sex education classes in school. I had no idea what sperm was or what an orgasm was. I was taught that sex was bad, that it was dirty, and it was only done to create babies. I was told that masturbation was evil and blowjobs were for whores. It is no surprise that I developed a great deal of fear and negative judgments about sex.

When I finally had my first sexual experience, I felt guilty and ashamed because I enjoyed it and wanted more. My experience was that sex was intoxicatingly delightful, yet my programming was that sex was bad and wrong. It was difficult for those opposites to coexist in me, and this created a great deal of inner conflict for me.

Eventually, I came to understand that my mother's negative attitudes about sex were due to her pain. I also came to understand that her motive for instilling in me a negative view of sex was her way of protecting me from experiencing the same pain she had experienced in this area of her life. I recognized that I did not have to adopt her attitudes; that her life and path were not mine. I could create my own view of sex based on my own experiences instead of on hers.

I began learning about my body – what I liked, what felt good, where my G spot was, and so on. I had been learning to love and accept myself, and now I wanted to embrace my sexuality. I did not like having negative judgments about sex, so I starting learning everything I could about having a healthy, sexual relationship – with my husband and with myself.

I immersed myself in educational books and TV shows about sex. These tools helped me see sex in a completely different way – as healthy and normal. They helped me let go of the guilt, shame, and fear I had associated with sexual intimacy. They also gave me a lot of things to ponder, explore, and practice.

Challenging my sexual programming opened me up to the beauty and sacredness of sex. I was able to release my fear, shame, guilt, and negative judgments. Breaking free of the negative associations imposed upon me by others, I have been able to allow Divine sexual energy to flow through me. I have also been able to assist other women in finding their freedom, through my Goddess workshops, Goddess Circles, and hypnosis.

Many of us have developed negative associations with sex – some from childhood programming, some from experiences of violation or exploitation. No matter the root cause, it is possible for us to heal these negative associations and begin to enjoy sexual intimacy.

Sex is meant to be enjoyed, to create pleasure. It is not something to be afraid of. Sex is not bad, dirty, or intended only for 'whores', as my upbringing suggested. It is a natural, healthy, and normal way to connect with and give love to the one we hold special in our hearts. It is an expression of love and intimacy.

There are many styles of sexual intimacy, and we can learn to fully embrace and express our sexual selves. When we resolve the shame or guilt we may hold about sex, and when we begin to love and respect ourselves, we can create deliciously wonderful sexual experiences.

By incorporating sensuality and our senses, we can experience magnificent sex that can leave us feeling like we are floating on a magical cloud. We can easily stimulate our desires through our senses, such as wearing sexy lingerie for pleasuring sight and touch; giving gentle massages to one another, caressing our partner's body from head to toe for tactile pleasure; listening to music that has a slow, erotic tempo which can make us move in a way that synchronizes each thrust with each beat; applying essential oils or perfumes to enhance the romantic atmosphere, and including flavors to taste, such as chocolate or whipped cream. Focusing on our senses can enhance foreplay and the added stimulation can heighten arousal, making sex even more enjoyable for both parties.

Sacred Sexuality

"Let everything we do and say be an expression of the beauty in our heart, always based on LOVE."   *- Don Miguel Ruiz*

Sexual intimacy is an important part of committed relationships. Sex can be enjoyable as just the physical act; however it can become a sacred act if we take the time to be present with our partners.

For sex to be the sacred gift of a physical expression of love, it is wise to be mindful of a few things. Society has taught us many versions of "appropriate" and "inappropriate" sex. There are no "rules" beyond mutual consent and respect. The important thing is that we treat our partners and their bodies with respect, and insist that our partners do the same with us.

Some things to consider in a sacred sexual relationship include:

1. **Connection is the primary objective.** Connection and intimacy are the goals in a sacred sexual relationship, not sex. Connection and intimacy may lead to sex, but sex itself is not the goal. Being intimate with our partners – being present, connecting with our hearts, having good eye contact, kissing, caressing, and cherishing each moment – creates a space of emotional safety that allows both partners to open their hearts to each other. Feeling connected to each other keeps each partner coming back for more pleasure. When we create an intimate relationship with our partners, we communicate that they are important to us. By taking time to be focused and present with our partners, we can connect on deeper levels. By being present, we can cherish the sacred moment of this experience. No matter the frequency of sex with our partners, each experience is its own, and no two encounters are the same. When we are present, we get to experience each encounter as the once-in-a-lifetime moment it truly is. Being present allows us to silence our "mind chatter" which can distract us from the intimate energy. By using all our senses to explore one another, we can enhance our pleasure and our partners' pleasure. We can focus our attention on all of our

senses during these sacred experiences. We can look into each other's eyes as we pay attention to our partners' breathing and movements and notice the feel of our partners' breath on our bodies. We can make love to each other by exploring each other's bodies in a gentle, sensual way, enjoying the process of making love instead of rushing to get the orgasm. This is not a race. We can take the time to do things we know our partners enjoy, such as caressing, holding, passionately kissing, or stimulating his or her G spots. By being present in these actions, we can enjoy the spiritual connection as well as the physical connection.

2. **Pay attention to the energy.** During sexual intercourse, partners not only share their bodies, they share their energy. Energy is exchanged between partners during sex, so making sure our energy is clear is a gift of love for our partners. By clearing our energy fields ahead of time, sexual intimacy can become a healing and balancing experience. If we are feeling low or having a bad day, we should do something that creates balance for us before engaging in sexual activity – such as a walk in nature, working out, meditating, or smudging with sage. If we are not energetically balanced, our low energy may negatively affect our partner's energy, as well as the sexual interaction.

3. **Honor instead of objectifying.** To create a sacred sexual relationship, partners need to treat each other as equals, not as objects for sexual gratification. Objectification makes a person

feel used and is not healthy for any relationship. Treating each other with respect, being kind, and sharing sacred love with our partners communicates appreciation for our partners and our relationship, which will allow our relationships to grow stronger, healthier, and lead to a long- lasting relationship. Honoring each other and remembering we are more than just our bodies makes this a sacred experience.

4. **Hygiene is an act of respect.** Having a clean body is important when preparing to make love. When we take the time to clean ourselves and our intimate areas, replacing the sweat and dirt of the day with fresh-smelling skin, we show our partner respect. Our sense of smell is heightened during sex. If our bodies are clean, both parties can more fully enjoy, caress, and explore without the distraction of unpleasant smells. Everyone has a natural smell, and some partners prefer the smell of natural pheromones, but clean genitals smell and taste better, allowing both partners to give and receive oral pleasure and explore each other without any distractions. We wash lettuce before making a salad, so why wouldn't we wash our own delicacies before serving them to someone we love? Much like getting ready for a first date, we want to make sure we are prepared and clean so we can be at our best. Taking time to groom – our teeth, hair, and entire body – sends the message that our relationships and partners are worth the extra time and effort we put into ourselves, and our partners will appreciate this simple act.

5. **Communicate.** None of us are mind-readers, so it is important to maintain open communication with our partners. Sometimes one partner will want to engage in a particular activity. Although the other partner doesn't, he or she will go along with the activity to make the other person happy. This actually harms the relationship rather than strengthening it. Both partners must be in agreement. Engaging in an act that one doesn't really want to do is emotional abandonment of the self – sacrificing one's needs for the approval of another. Both partners need to feel safe expressing him or herself. Both need to feel safe setting boundaries without fear of rejection or retaliation. Sometimes a partner may have a difficult time stating preferences due to past wounds; however the body cannot lie. If a partner's body language begins telling us something, such as he or she is not enjoying him or herself, we must pay attention to it. We can ask questions – ask if it is alright to do certain things, and ask how the partner feels. Making sure that both partners are fully enjoying this sacred experience is very important to ensuring a lasting and loving relationship. This sacred connection has to be enjoyable for the both partners. Everyone is different. It is important that we take the time to learn our partner's sexual language and communicate ours to him or her. If one feels shy about sharing his or her desires and preferences, this needs to be explored, as this is evidence of fear. Both partners need to be able to trust and express themselves freely to the other.

Try some of these suggestions next time you are with your partner. Communicate and be honest with your partner. Notice any negative thoughts you have about sex and gently challenge them. Remember, sex is not bad; it's the expression of love for one another.

Connecting in a way that will use all of your senses will increase your electrical magnetic field. It can be very healing to have regular sacred sex. It can heighten your sensitivity and increase your sensuality, it pumps endorphins in your body, and it's also a great workout!

I had a question presented to me once: "What if you don't like your partner or don't respect them. What if you don't find your mate attractive or interesting?" There are a surprising number of people in these situations. Awareness is a good first step; however, action needs to follow.

If we do not feel a connection to a partner, or are not happy in our relationship, maintaining the status quo will be energetically draining and sexual intimacy will not be very pleasurable. Our hearts will ache, and the relationship will become empty and shallow – a relationship of lust instead of a relationship of love.

If we don't find a way to shift the energy, the relationship will become an energetic burden. We will start feeling "out of sorts." We may begin to feel lost, upset, or anxious. Paying attention to our feelings and being honest with ourselves is very important. We can't remain in an unfulfilling relationship simply because we have children, or our partners financially support us, or because we are scared to leave. If we lack real love in our relationship, we need to explore within ourselves and do something that will create a healthier relationship, or make some other change that will honor ourselves and our partners. We ought never to let fear hold us back from finding a true sacred connection with another. Sex is not everything, but it's a big part of having a healthy, sacred relationship and sharing ourselves in the most divine and open way possible with a partner.

It is imperative that we make the time to take care of ourselves and nurture the goddess within. We must listen to our bodies and pay attention to all our senses. We can do a personal inventory of our relationships by asking: "How do I feel when I am sexually involved with my partner? Is it something I enjoy? Or is it an obligation?"

We need to stay connected to our hearts and honor what it tells us. Sexual intimacy ought to be something we look forward to, as it is an experience that can bring us into full bliss. We can be in full union with our divine light and create an energy that will surround us for days. Sex should not be a chore. We should enjoy the sacred process and intimate connection.

Connecting Through Our Senses

We can use our senses as a way to connect with Source. Nature is sacred, and being present with the nature we have around us can help us feel grounded and to feel God's presence. Many cultures have practiced connecting to Source through nature for generations; however our society doesn't think much about it.

For years, I was a part of a sacred woman's circle, which practiced Native traditions. Through these monthly gatherings, I learned a lot about earth-based spirituality. I learned that Nature has energy that we can connect to at any time.

In our gatherings, we used herbs and plants such as sage, cedar, and sweet grass to smudge our bodies and clear our energy fields. Smudging incorporated our sense of smell to heal and balance our energy fields.

We also made traditional hand drums using deer hide, and learned about drum medicine. Listening to the beats of the drum is like connecting to the heartbeat of Mother Earth and can be a very healing experience. Connecting to Source through our sense of sound, to the beat of the drum, calms our nervous system and recharges our batteries.

Basking in the sun and feeling the sun's warmth on our skin is a great way of connecting with Source through the sense of touch. The energy from the sun provides a sort of nourishment. Animals and plants will seek out the sun for the energy it provides. Animals will constantly change their location to bask in the rays, while plants will change the direction of growth in order to access the energy.

Touch, Sound, Taste, Smell: What a Sight - Oh My!

Sometimes we may find that it is very easy to get lost in our busy lives and tight schedules. We need to remember to connect with our senses, slow down, and take time to explore our surroundings. Being present in our surroundings creates a balance in our lives. We need to remember to pay attention to what's happening around us and listen to our hearts. When we practice focusing on our senses and living in awareness of our surroundings, we become less stressed about the little things. We may feel more connected to one sense, but we can practice being mindful of each sense on a daily basis. This helps develop sensuality, which in turn creates more pleasure for us.

Right now, stop for just a moment and feel, see, taste, smell, and hear what is surrounding you. Feel the support of the seat under you – the firmness or softness and the comfort. See the detail in fabric near you – the weave, the texture, and the color variances. Taste the drink beside you, your lips, or notice the taste in your mouth. Smell the air. What subtle scents do you notice: perfume, freshly shampooed hair, essential oils or food? Listen to the sounds around you – birds outside, traffic, the refrigerator or heater running.

Opening ourselves up to the universe in a sensual way allows us to experience things like magic. Remember – Show up fully. Each day you are given an opportunity to be present and to connect heart to heart. Explore your senses and enjoy.

Touch

We are sensual beings who like to feel good. Using all of our senses can help us achieve that. Having awareness of our sense of touch is a great tool in helping us heal. Our skin is the largest organ and has millions of nerve endings, making it a very easy way to enjoy our sense of touch.

Physical touch stimulates our brain to produce natural endorphins that help us feel better. We need to touch things that make our bodies feel good. Maybe it's petting a dog or cuddling with our children on the soft sofa, watching a family movie. Or it can be receiving or giving a massage or a long hug. Gently taking time to honor our bodies by doing some yoga or exercising can bring awareness to our sense of touch, as we are using our bodies in a way that makes us feel good, stimulating our sense of touch with each move.

The sense of touch connects us to each other. It makes us feel secure, happy, and loved. We can see it in our children when they have had a bad day at school, and we just want to give them a hug. Our hug communicates that we are here for them and that we care. A hug will make anyone feel better, if they accept it. The energy connection we get when we are embracing in a hug is something that can heal and balance us.

Physical touch is extremely important for everyone. It helps each of us balance our physical and emotional states of being. Studies have shown that if a child does not receive adequate loving human contact, even if all of his physical needs are met, his brain will be affected, and he can develop long-term mental and emotional problems, or even die.

I am known for my big bear hugs. To me, it's a great way to spread love to others. I like to imagine the energy of a hug as an instant love bubble. To connect with someone heart-to-heart, just might be the medicine that they need at that moment. I know I feel better with a big, long hug, connecting to the sacred space of our hearts. I am not a one-second hugger that just holds a blink-long embrace and gives a pat on the back so lightly. I am the heart-to-heart, big squeeze-type hugger. I like to make sure the person I am hugging feels held, supported, and loved.

Next time you are about to hug someone say to yourself, "I want to connect with this person heart-to-heart and place an instant love bubble around him or her." This will keep you present in your sense of touch, which in turn is very healing.

We can even use visualization techniques to stimulate our sense of touch. One of my favorite visualizations is a Water Visualization. I use it to ground and center by staying present with the water during a shower. This visualization exercises our sense of touch, by focusing on our skin as we feel the water all over our bodies.

Water Visualization

Go take a long, warm shower. Be fully present. Feel the water pouring on your body. Feel the temperature of the water. Notice how your body feels as the water flows. Embrace the sensation of the water.

Water symbolizes the emotional body; so begin to let go of the emotions stored in the tissues of your body. As the water hits an area of your body, notice if there is any tension or tightness there. Imagine a tight knot beginning to loosen, and allow the tension in that part of your body to release. Allow the water to hit every different part of your body that may hold any tension.

Imagine knots loosening, and allow the tension to release. Imagine any pockets of anger or sadness or other unpleasant feelings begin to dissolve and wash away as the water flows. See all the emotions of the day melt away down your arms and legs and out through the tips of your fingers and toes. These emotions may appear as colors, such as black or grey, and as they wash away, the colors may fade until the water runs clear in that area.

Feel the water coming down your head and shoulders, all the way down your upper body, and then down your lower body.

Notice all your muscles becoming loose and relaxed as your body becomes cleansed of the constricting emotions it had been storing.

Imagine, also, that the water is clearing your energy field. As you pay attention to where the water is landing on your body, notice how your energy becoming lighter, stronger, and clearer. Anything that was bothering you has been washed down the drain, returning to Mother Earth where it is blessed and transmuted.

Once you feel balanced and cleared, thank the water, and then continue with your shower as you normally would.

Pay Attention – I Can Never Say This Enough

Start observing your body. Notice what makes you feel good and what are you experiencing while you are feeling good. What sense is your strongest sense, meaning what sense brings you more awareness and more pleasure? It's beneficial to you if you start enhancing all your senses by slowing down in your daily activities and being present in each moment as much as you can.

Take deeper breaths, feeling your lungs expand, smelling the freshness of the air around you. Notice how after just 3 deep breaths, you begin to feel calmer and lighter.

When eating, turn off any distractions and be with your food – really taste the flavors, feel the textures, and notice your body's response to the food you are consuming. Notice at what point you become bored with the food and are no longer savoring it and eating becomes just an activity. Notice if you really want to eat the food or if you're just eating it because it is there.

When you are getting a hug from someone, feel the body pressed against yours, feel the embrace as it wraps around your neck or waist, notice the warmth of the body as life flows through him or her, and notice the scent of perfume, soap, or skin. Feel the energy of love and connection enveloping and filling your body with love.

When you are listening to you favorite music, try to isolate the instruments and hear their individual contribution to the song, feel the beat of the bass, move your body to the beat, feel the music touching your soul.

Where ever you are, look around you and find something that is beautiful. It may be a piece of art, a tree, a bird, mountains, children playing, a couple in love, or even an act of kindness.

Next time you are at the beach, take off your shoes and slide your feet into the sand. Try to feel each grain of sand on the bottom of your soles and in between your toes. The warmth of the sand is like a magical blanket that can transport us back into peace. It can remind us that we can change our mood at any time by connecting to our feelings and embracing the sense of touch. It's very grounding to feel Mother Nature on our skin. Standing on the earth with bare feet is like having an energy boost for our souls.

We are like rechargeable batteries. We can go long periods of time energized and balanced, but sooner or later, we will need to connect to a higher energy source: our Source. Connecting to Source through our senses is exactly how we can recharge our batteries of life. Plugging into the unlimited power of the universe is a great way to stay fully charged. When we are fully charged, we can uplift and energize others and create a movement of positive energy all around us.

Sound

Paying attention to the sounds in our environment is a great way to connect with our surroundings and practice being present. Sounds are vibrations interpreted by our brains through our ears. Different sounds have different vibrational frequencies and have different affects on us. Some sounds, such as sounds in nature – birds, water sources, frogs and even children laughing – make us feel happy and uplifted, while other sounds, such as honking cars or heavy metal music, can make us feel stressed and irritated. When the vibrations of sounds and our personal vibrations interact, they create either resonance or interference. Sound can, therefore, have a positive or negative impact on us.

Listening to something that makes us connect to a happy memory is a way to use our sense of sound to heal ourselves. Soft relaxing spa music helps us unwind and relax. Listening to positive affirmations or upbeat music before an interview can help us feel more confident and positive and improve our performance in the interview. Connecting to the sound of our breath helps us center and balance ourselves – breathing in relaxation and breathing out frustrations. Nature is also very musical and can assist in relaxing. Listening to the gentleness of nature's dance is a great way to let go and be present. The birds, the wind, and the oceans waves all have the power to shift our energy fields if we let them.

Music has been around for centuries and is found in every culture around the world. It can help us feel better, feel worse, feel happy, feel excitement, feel fear, and so on. When we watch TV, we can notice the sounds that are playing in the background. Is it a romantic song during a love scene? Are the sounds making our heartbeat faster during a mystery show or chase scene? Are there animal sounds? Waterfalls? Heavy metal? Jazz? The movie industry knows how music affects us and uses it to subtly effect our emotions as we watch the images.

Sound is measured in cycles per second, called hertz (Hz). The frequency of 8 Hz is said to be the fundamental "beat" of the planet, or "the heartbeat of Earth" which brings the biomolecular system and brain into balance. Sounds in nature have the frequency of 432 Hz, which is the natural frequency of the universe. Music based on 432 Hz transmits healing energy because it is a pure tone of the mathematics fundamental to nature. Each chakra has its own natural frequency, as well, which is why we can "feel" a Tibetan singing bowl or crystal bowl in our bodies as it plays.

Sounds can be very healing and can be used by practitioners to assist in our healing journeys. Tibetan chimes or bowls can be used to clear the energy of a space as well as a person. A crystal bowl concert can fill the room with a high-vibration frequency that can leave everyone feeling revitalized and energized. Music can shift our energy and help us let go of lower-vibration thoughts and worries.

Listening to music can help heal us by shifting our energy fields. Giving us more energy or assisting us in releasing energy. Music impacts our moods and can put us in the mood to exercise, to dance, to relax, and to sleep. It is a great way to fully express ourselves, whether we are playing or listening. Even if we don't speak the same language, we can still understand what the song is about by the way it makes us feel. Music can help us relax after a long, busy day. Music can help us meditate, taking us into a deeper level of awareness. Music can enliven us, giving us energy to work out.

If we have pent up emotions, such as sadness, and we want to release them, listening to something that makes us feel sad can allow us to fully embrace and feel our feelings of sadness.

After a few songs, we can then listen to something that is more uplifting and connects us to the divine flow of Source – something that fills us with positivity and makes us feel good.

We must let go of self-judgment and create a sacred space of being in the vibrational sounds we need at any time. It is very healing to accept and allow any emotions we are experiencing – to let them pass through, without resistance, just letting them flow and letting them go.

Feel your emotions and be one with it. Did you know tears of sadness vs. tears of joy are chemically different? Yes, our bodies create the exact concoction we need at any time for healing to take place. Let go of the fear to express your feelings. Let the tears flow. Give yourself permission to express yourself as you are. Feel it. Be it. Release it.

Use your senses to help you heal, transform and embrace your Inner Goddess. Nurture the Divine Feminine within. We each are made of both masculine and feminine energy. Nurturing and allowing things to come up is a way you can express your Divine Feminine. Balance is key, if you are always going and doing, such as in the Divine Masculine, make sure to schedule in time to pause, reflect and nurture your feminine side.

Sometimes we may need to be in our masculine side more then in our feminine side. To reach deadlines, accomplish goals and take action. Listen to your body and your inner guidance system; it truly knows how to steer you. The feminine side creates, nurtures and brings forth dreams. The masculine side takes the steps needed to bring your dreams into reality, by taking action. It is truly a dance. A dance of compassion, love, intuition, power, determination and drive. Remember to be gentle with yourself, take each step mindfully and listen to your heart. Find your balance.

Asking For What You Want

Anything that makes us feel pleasure with our senses is sensual. Maybe you like hearing words that are appealing to you, such as erotic talk. In my Goddess workshops, I encourage my guests to own their voices and speak up for what they desire. If they want their partners to do something, I encourage them to express it to their partners. Words can be very empowering and liberating at the same time. Erotic talk is a fun way to communicate sexual desires while engaging the imagination to increase sensuality.

For many, erotic talk is uncomfortable. Many of us were raised to feel that anything related to sex is dirty and for "bad girls" and that erotic talk – or "talking dirty" – is inappropriate, myself included. But as I grew into the person I am today, I learned to let go of those negative, fear-based teachings. I began to understand that these beliefs had been instilled in me with the intent to keep me from becoming a promiscuous teen. I chose to challenge those limiting beliefs as an adult, and start embracing myself fully as a sensual and sexual being, just as God had intended for me to be.

I began using words that brought pleasure into my life and discovered that they enhanced and brought more fun and communication to sexual interactions with my husband. It was a giant leap outside of my comfort zone when I first began to do this, however the benefit of intimate communication through erotic talk far outweighed the initial discomfort. I was able to ask for what I precisely wanted in a way that prevented experiencing sexual frustration on my part and risking a bruised ego on his part.

You can start experimenting with the power of words to increase your sensual side by simply completing the following sentences during intimate moments:

"It feels good when you ...."
"You make me feel so ...."
"I really like your ...."
"I want you to ...."
"It is so hot when you ...."

Making sounds during lovemaking is beneficial in expressing yourself fully. It communicates to your partner that you are enjoying this sacred experience, thus giving your partner confidence that he/she is doing a good job satisfying you.

Taste

Taste is a powerful sense; just look at all the different types of restaurants around. There is something for everyone. The sense of taste can be very pleasurable for most of us. As humans we seek out pleasure, and the flavors of various foods can provide us with a sense of peace, comfort, happiness, and delight.

There is a natural reaction in our bodies when we take a bite of something delicious. Our taste buds react and send messages to our brain, which, in turn, releases endorphins, the pleasure chemical. Our cells record the information, and we are drawn to the food again and again.

Next time you eat, pay attention to each flavor you experience. Close your eyes and really taste the food. Chew it slowly to release all the juices it may hold. Allow each bite to travel across your tongue and touch each taste bud. Notice any sensations in your body as your taste buds react to the flavors. Notice what messages your body may be giving you. How do you feel as you eat this food? Is it satisfying your hunger? Or is it satisfying your boredom? Or are you eating for fuel or because you are stressed out? Notice your body's emotional response to the food. Really start paying attention to what you are consuming, and pay attention to the energy you feel after eating.

Using our sense of taste can become a meditation practice. By paying attention to each bite or drink, we can be present and mindful and expand our awareness, thereby increasing our connection to Source.

The sense of taste can also enhance our feelings of sexual pleasure and provide sexual energy through the flavors and emotional effects of different foods. We know them as aphrodisiac foods, such as dark chocolate, oysters, whipped cream, bananas, and cherries, just to name a few. Melting chocolate and eating it with bananas, or maybe even pouring the warm chocolate on our lovers' body, is a fun way to explore and enjoy our sense of taste and can spike arousal.

Sniff, Sniff

Our sense of smell is another powerful sense we have that can help us connect to ourselves fully. We can experience great pleasure through our sense of smell. Different scents have different affects on us, and some are strongly associated to our memories.

The beautiful scents of the flowers, the strong smell of the cedar trees, and the earthy scent of a coming rainstorm can have a calming, peaceful effect on us. The scent of fresh-baked bread or cookies can feel comforting. The freshness of a baby's skin can make us feel love and joy. The unique scent of our partner can be like an aphrodisiac – a delightful scent that makes us long for his/her embrace.

Our sense of smell can change our state of being. The scent of lavender can help us relax, while the scent of peppermint can invigorate us. Perfumes can also affect our moods, making us feel good, confident, or sexy.

By paying attention to the effects certain smells have on us, we can become more in tune with ourselves. We can notice what emotions certain scents stir in us. By being present with the smells around us, we can increase our awareness and practice being present, thereby connecting to our Source.

Essential oils and herbs have been used for thousands of years to assist in healing. I love burning incense and creating an atmosphere of relaxation for myself after a busy day. Try using oils and natural scented candles to set the stage for romance when you are about to be intimate with yourself or your partner. I know when my husband takes extra time to set up the room for us; it really shows me he cares. It makes me feel extra special, and the romantic atmosphere just feels better. It takes me out of the mom archetype and into the lover archetype. Explore your sense of smell; use the gifts of the universe to embrace yourself fully.

Sight

Sight is a sense that can vary from person to person. We can view the same thing, but see it completely differently. Our judgments and perceptions affect the way we see things without us even knowing it. We need to be mindful of the attitude we carry so we can fully enjoy the beauty around us. When we practice enjoying all the beauty around us, we can see how magical life truly is.

We can use sight to improve our attitude of gratitude. We can be present with what we are seeing in each moment and find something to appreciate about it. We can appreciate the golden glow cast across a field at sunrise or the varying shades of grey in a storm cloud. We can appreciate the intricate details of the center of a sunflower or a lady bug. We can appreciate the brightness that shines in the eyes of a happy baby or the rough and wrinkled skin of someone with a life long-lived. Each moment and each person or thing we lay our eyes on provides us an opportunity to find something to appreciate, which in turn, allows a deeper connection to Source.

Nature is full of colors – the bright colors of parrots, flowers, and butterflies are very appealing. Each color is a specific frequency and can be used to affect our energy fields and strengthen our chakras.

Scientific studies have been conducted that show how different colors affect us. Red is a strong color and suggests power, such as a red "power tie." Navy blue suggests trustworthiness and is often worn by defendants in high-profile court cases. Pastel green and blue are calming colors and are often found in primary schools, detention centers, and certain hospital wards.

Notice what color you are wearing right now. How does it make you feel? What colors do you most frequently wear? What colors do you avoid wearing? Why?

What we see affects our minds. Being aware of what we choose to look at is important for a healthy mind. We always have a choice of focusing on what brings us peace or what brings us fear. Positive images will help us feel uplifted and expanded, while negative images will make us feel heavy and constricted. We can all tell the difference in how we feel when we see something cute, like a baby, a puppy, or funny cat videos, and when we watch the news and see images of war, conflict, or violence. The images send our brain a message that creates an emotional response, which affects our physical bodies. Everything we see gets processed in our brains and implanted in our subconscious minds. Our bodies and subconscious minds do not know that these images are just images and respond as if these events are our own personal experiences. This is why a scary movie makes us nervous and jumpy and a sad movie makes us cry. Everything we see is processed as our personal realities and affects our minds, bodies, and energy. This is why it is important to pay attention to what we view and focus our attention on more positive images.

We can also use our imagination as a variation of sight. Visualizations are images in our minds that are created by our imagination instead of viewed by our eyes. Interestingly, the emotional and body affects are just as powerful. Again, our subconscious minds and bodies don't know if what we are "seeing" is an experience or a mere image. We can use this to our advantage and visualize positive situations, interactions, and outcomes to raise our vibrations and improve our experiences of life.

Because we are affected by what we see, it is important to be mindful of our environments. If our homes or office spaces are cluttered, the clutter can have a negative effect on us, while organized spaces will have a positive effect. Decluttering makes us feel more relaxed and at ease. It allows us to enjoy our spaces without the stress of looking for something or feeling the pressure of needing to clean up. An organized space can increase productivity and provide a space – energetically and physically – for us to begin life-enhancing projects that can further increase our positive energy.

Our sense of sight is a beautiful gift; a gift that we can use in so many ways to connect us to ourselves and Source in powerful ways. Even using our intuition is a form of sight. Our intuition is our inner knowing, our inner guidance system. Trust your intuition and listen to your divine guidance. It will always lead you in the right direction.

Being a Goddess means you give yourself permission to blossom. You trust the journey, you honor your gifts and you stay open to receive Love. By listening to your calling and inner knowing you will live a happier and more fulfilling life.

Writing this book has assisted me in more ways than I could have imagined. I am grateful for the opportunity to share my journey with you. I would love to hear about your journey and support you as you continue unfolding into the beautiful and powerful Goddess that you are.

With Love,
Natalie